CORRUPTION UNVEILED:

A Historical Investigation Into The Collapse of Great Civilizations

BOOK I

ABBEY ABRAMSON

DEDICATION

To my parents, siblings, and family, who have been my life support, and to all my friends and mentors in all walks of life.

CONTENTS

CHAPTER 1.

UNDERSTANDING CORRUPTION

Corruption is an omnipresent and complex social reality that has existed across societies and civilizations for millennia down to the modern world. In broader terms, corruption includes a spectrum of unlawful acts and behaviors that can sabotage the integrity of various societies, cultures, organizations, institutions, or states in which an individual or group engages. Some societies may consider something not necessarily illegal or unlawful, but the same behavior may be immoral or unethical to the perception of others.

Corruption is debilitating as it can negatively affect development, political stability, national security, environment and nature, climate change, social equity, and cultural norms. Therefore, corruption should be tackled by qualified individuals or authorities with a multidimensional approach critical to comprehending corruption thoroughly. Such an approach should include exploring historical facts and events, manifestations, definitions, and implications, which demands intellectual curiosity and engagement.

What is Corruption?

Corruption is broadly perceived and understood as the abuse of power for personal, political, and corporate gain. It is generally defined as involving the misuse and abuse of public office, private sector authority, or any position of trust to secure advantages, benefits, and wealth, often at the expense of public or organizational interest. From a high-ranking government official to an ordinary worker, anyone at all levels in society can commit corruption. Aside from financial gain and other personal securities, corruption can involve pursuing other benefits, such as political influence, social status, more authority, and power, or worse, evading justice and lawful punishment.

Faces of Corruption

Corruption manifests in multifarious forms, each with distinct and related characteristics, impacts, intensity, and consequences. While some forms are blatant and detectable, some are opaque and highly challenging to discover and detect. This introductory chapter explores the most typical forms of corruption, including bribery, embezzlement, fraud, extortion, nepotism, cronyism, patronage, influence peddling, and kickback.

Bribery

Bribery is the most pervasive, dominant, familiar, and traditional form of corruption. Essentially, it demands the exchange, offer, receipt, or solicitation of something valuable to influence the decisions or actions of someone with authority or in a position of influence. This unlawful and unethical practice, at least in most societies past and present, is a typical activity in the business world, public services, law enforcement, and political environment. A company offering a massive bribe to a government official for preferential treatment in obtaining a lucrative public contract or a traffic police officer accepting money from a motorist caught violating the traffic rules are some examples of bribery activities.

Embezzlement

Embezzlement manifests in dishonest appropriation or withholding of funds or property entrusted to an authority or group in a high position. As a white-collar crime, embezzlement is typically committed by a public official or an employee exploiting public resources for personal gain. A high-ranking government official commits embezzlement by siphoning off public funds into an individual account. Obviously, this illegal practice frequently occurs in public institutions, civic organizations, welfare centers, financial institutions, and banks.

Fraud

Third is a fraudulent act. Fraud encompasses and goes beyond calculated deception or misrepresentation, intending to obtain unfair and unlawful benefits. Fraud involves manipulating information, falsifying records, and other dishonest practices. A typical example of fraud is the act of submitting falsified expense reports to obtain reimbursement for personal expenses. Probably, this was also prevalent among tax collectors in the past great civilizations, wherein they excessively collected tax from peasants and submitted reports to the empire but pocketed the difference.

Extortion

Extortion is quite different among corrupt acts as it could involve not only mental or emotional but also physical violence in extreme cases. It uses force by unlawfully demanding or receiving money or something of value, often through (physical or psychological) threats or coercion. This corrupt activity prevails when power is concentrated in a few hands or individuals, making it difficult for victims to resist. For example, a government official might demand a bribe from a business owner in exchange for not shutting down their business, or a gang extorting protection money from a shopkeeper.

Nepotism and Cronyism

These corrupt twins involve favoritism based on relationships rather than merit. In particular, nepotism is the practice of giving jobs or unfair advantages to family members and close relatives, while cronyism involves preferring friends or close associates over outsiders in one's circle. However, both nepotistic and cronyistic practices undermine fairness and equal opportunities for qualified individuals to land a job position. These practices have direct negative impacts, such as inefficiencies in government institutions and corporations, ultimately ailing governance and failing businesses.

More often than not, nepotism and cronyism are less visible and challenging to detect but can negatively impact the efficiency of institutions. For example, a nepotist chief executive officer or chairperson hires an unqualified family member for a high-level position, bypassing more qualified candidates and ignoring the merit-based hiring process. This undignified practice can lead to inefficient governmental functions and reduce morale among other employees.

Patronage

Patronage (from the root word 'patron,' meaning sponsor or guarantor) involves granting favors, contracts, or appointments in exchange for political backing. It is frequently utilized to strengthen one's authority and influence political structures, often resulting in pervasive deterioration within the governmental system. A classic example of patronage occurs through allocating government contracts to business allies or individuals based on their political adherence to relatively fair competition, such as bidding. Many perpetrators exploit patronage to secure a political position or job by tapping on their family or individual connections to whom they acted as godparents or patrons, such as at weddings, christenings, or baptisms.

Influence Peddling

Influence peddling happens when one leverages authority or connections to exploit decision-makers and obtain favors and preferential treatment. Influence peddling is a common practice in political and business fields, where accessing influential figures is often seen as a valuable commodity and a speedy method to achieve quick benefits. A familiar example of influence peddling is when a company executive uses their connections with government officials, disregarding fair and transparent processes to secure lucrative government contracts and projects.

Kickback

A kickback is a bargained form of bribery via negotiations. It is accomplished by contracting a portion or other financial transaction proceeds and then illicitly returned to the person who facilitated the deal. Kickbacks are extremely hard to detect as they are often disguised within legal transactions in any legal business activity. Kickbacks are challenging to detect in many industries, including government contracting, construction, grand projects, and healthcare. For example, in the healthcare industry, a pharmaceutical company might offer a kickback to a healthcare ministry in exchange for prescribing their medications to patients suffering from polio or COVID-19. Kickbacks can lead to over-prescription and increased healthcare costs, compromising the quality of care and overall public health. Therefore, according to law, the perpetrators must be legally punished due to the legal and ethical implications that distort the fair competition and integrity of business transactions.

The Impact of Corruption

Corruption is a global pressing matter. It is one of the significant culprits of poverty, inequality, social unrest, environmental degradation, and other devastating long-term consequences. Corruption erodes the trust of citizens in institutions, weakens governance, stifles economic development, harms the environment, and aggravates climate change issues. Historical cases show widespread corruption can lead (or has led) to the collapse of societies, governments, empires, and great civilizations (see Chapters 3-5).

Diverting resources from fundamental public services such as healthcare, education, food, housing, and other major public development projects is one of the major red flags of corruption. Diversion of resources and finances exacerbates poverty, inequality, the rich and poor gap, social unrest, environmental degradation, and climate change issues. Corruption undermines the rule of law by allowing individuals and entities to evade accountability through varied corrupt practices aforementioned. Corruption can hinder economic growth by creating barriers to entry of necessary goods, increasing the cost of doing business, diverting project finances, and encouraging the allocation of resources based on connections rather than merit in the private sector.

Corruption also negatively impacts effective political and governance processes and systems. Severe acts of corruption can irreparably hurt democratic systems by subverting electoral processes, manipulating legislation, blocking bipartisan policy dialogue, and eroding public trust in duly elected public representatives. In authoritarian regimes, corruption is often used to maintain control and suppress dissent, further embedding the power of the ruling demagogue. Autocrats bribe the police to easily control people who try to protest, push more democratic systems, and demand social justice and accountability.

Legal and Moral Dimensions

Corruption is not only a legal issue but also an ethical one. In the legal sphere, corruption is defined and penalized under diverse and standard national and international laws. These laws can prevent and punish corrupt practices through criminal sanctions, civil penalties, and administrative measures.

International conventions, such as the United Nations Convention against Corruption (UNCAC) and the Organization for Economic Cooperation and Development (OECD) Anti-Bribery Convention, are globalized standards for fighting corruption.

The moral dimensions of corruption go beyond legal definitions. Corruption has moral dimensions that go beyond legal definitions of the term. Corruption raises questions on fairness, equality, justice, and accountability of individuals in higher positions granted. Additionally, corruption erodes the integrity of entrusted officers and/or institutions, questioning the values that sustain the cohesion of society. Moral philosophers and ethicists have been studying the nature of corruption and generally consider it not only a violation of legal norms but also a violation of moral duty and social responsibility by authorities.

The ethical ramifications of corrupt behavior are not only harmful but also deeply extensive to society and the system they are relying on. An unethical and immoral behavior can breed cynicism, erode civic virtue and trust, and damage social cohesion. Corruption can lead to a culture of impunity, where unethical behavior is tolerated and expected when it becomes normalized and widespread.

Worst of all, perpetrators can live freely without punishment and accountability for their actions. Corruption breeds moral decay and has lasting impacts and changes on the nature and psyche of a society. It weakens trust and cooperation among citizens, which are critical for social order, human development, nature conservation, and socioeconomic progress.

References

Glaeser, E. L., & Goldin, C. (Eds.). (2006). *Corruption and Reform: Lessons from America's Economic History*. University of Chicago Press.

Heywood, P. M. (Ed.). (2015). *Routledge Handbook of Political Corruption*. Routledge.

Johnston, M. (2005). *Syndromes of Corruption: Wealth, Power, and Democracy*. Cambridge University Press.

Klitgaard, R. (1988). *Controlling Corruption*. University of California Press.

Pope, J. (Ed.). (2000). *Confronting Corruption: The Elements of a National Integrity System*. Transparency International.

Rose-Ackerman, S., & Palifka, B. J. (2016). *Corruption and Government: Causes, Consequences, and Reform* (2nd ed.). Cambridge University Press.

Svensson, J. (2005). *Eight Questions about Corruption*. Journal of Economic Perspectives, 19(3), 19–42.

The World Bank. (1997). *Helping Countries Combat Corruption: The Role of the World Bank.*

Transparency International. (2020). *Global Corruption Barometer 2020.*

UNODC (United Nations Office on Drugs and Crime). (2004). United Nations Convention against Corruption (UNCAC).

Essay on Corruption in India: Historical, Types, & Examples. https://www.educba.com/essay-on-corruption-in-india/

CHAPTER 2.

ORIGINS AND EVOLUTION OF CORRUPTION

2.1. Early Human Societies and Corruption

We can track the origins of corruption in early human society even long before the ascent of the known civilizations and inscribed facts and records. When early humans turned from nomadic tribes of hunter-gatherers into more organized farming communities, power, resources, and distribution of goods changed utterly. These socio-economic transformations laid the foundation for the emergence of corruption. Corruption emerged as the authority of resources concentrated on a few individuals and groups who created opportunities strictly for themselves.

In this chapter, we will discover how corruption emerged in early human communities by exploring the socio-economic and environmental factors and elements that contributed to its emergence.

From Hunter-Gatherer to Agrarian Societies

Historical facts inform us that most early humans lived in small nomadic groups who lived through hunting, gathering, and grazing for survival. They lived as egalitarian groups, sharing work and resources equally among members whenever available. Somehow, the decision-making was collectively agreed upon, especially by leaders chosen based on consensus rather than wealth or status. The opportunities to be corrupt were minimal or nonexistent as they lacked accumulated resources or wealth. Besides, their close-knit relationship made it hard for any member to abuse their positions for exclusive gain (Service, 1975).

However, the pivotal turning point in human history emerged when the effective agricultural method developed at the beginning of 10,000 BCE during the Neolithic Revolution. At this stage, human societies established permanent settlements and accumulated ample resources as they became more adept in cultivating crops and domesticating or grazing animals. Their surplus produce allowed them to create more complex social hierarchies when some individuals or groups started controlling wider land tracks, more food stocks, and valuable goods than others. These social hierarchies laid the foundation for corruption to develop as the individuals or groups with more resources could use their authority and power to control the distribution of products, labor, and decision-making systems for their exclusive gain (Diamond, 1997).

The Birth of Social Hierarchies and Corruption

As the early agrarian communities advanced and became more complex, they established governing systems and social organizations. The systems logically picked leaders who were often from the most successful and influential families and began to wield power and control over their surrounding societies. These leaders have control and unfair advantage not only over the communities but also in agricultural production, managing shared resources, and decision-making on behalf of the community. In recognition of their work, these elites were specially granted privileges, such as receiving more shares of the produce and, better yet, control over vast livelihood resources like land and water (Service, 1975).

The potential for corruption was created as the concentration of power and control over resources were in the hands of these leaders. They could use their status to provide more for their relatives, allies, and loyalists at the expense of the larger community, such as allocating the fertile land and more livestock to their own families, leaving others with less productive options. The practices of favoritism subverted the expected trust of the community members in their leaders. Besides, favoritism eroded community cohesion, creating unfair livelihoods and a lack of opportunities for work and economic opportunities (Goody, 1976).

This form of corruption in early human societies was not confined to economic resources but also to the exercise of political power. When the condition of favoritism regarding land and resources grew worse, communities started showing common forms of grievances with the status quo. Complaints and personal grievances were voiced, but the leaders or elders who acted as judges in such disputes could be bribed or favor personal relationships, thus passing biased and unjust judgments. Above all, the absence of greater transparency systems was its blatant weakness that logically allowed the influential and powerful elites to act with impunity, further deeply ingrained corruption into the social fabric (Diamond, 1997).

Religion and Corruption in Early Societies

Religion played a central role in many early human societies, explaining natural phenomena, reinforcing social norms, and crucially legitimizing the authority of leaders. In many early human societies, religion played a critical function. It served as the means of explaining natural phenomena, reinforcing social norms, and even legitimizing the authority of leaders.

The shamans, priests and priestesses, spiritual leaders, and such religious leaders were often provided great respect and influence as they were thought to have access to the divine or have special knowledge, being the medium between the human and the spiritual world. While many religious leaders genuinely fulfilled their spiritual functions, on the other hand, some abused their influence by supporting the power of secular leaders or even controlling the beliefs and activities of the community (Service, 1975).

In some cases, the religious and political authorities have intertwined, creating greater avenues for corruption. Some influential religious leaders with control and access to sacred information or rituals could exploit their authority for personal gain, such as demanding more offerings (e.g., food or valuables) or favors in exchange for the religious services they only have the authority or power to perform. This form of religious authority exploitation has enriched the religious leaders and reinforced the social hierarchies by creating a system that obliged people to materially offer provisions to the religious elite (Graeber, 2011).

The alignment of religious and political power turned so deep that leaders or rules were worshipped as divine or at least semi-beings, strengthening their control over the lives of people and their resources in some early societies. The alignment and fusion of religious and secular powers often laid the foundation for the coalition of authority and wealth among the few elites. The fusion of powers and wealth in the hands of the few leaders exacerbated corruption and inequality in the society of this period. The abuse of the religious system in justifying corrupt behavior is more visible in later civilizations. However, its origins can be traced back to earlier human societies (Goody, 1976).

The Collapse of Early Societies

Assessing the long-term impacts of corruption in early human societies can be very challenging due to the limited archaeological and other recorded evidence available today. Nevertheless, it is possible to conjecture that corruption contributed to the rise and fall, collapse, or transformation of some early societies. The unfair practices by authorities and the loss of expected trust in leadership may have brought the vulnerability of communities to internal conflicts or external threats and aggressions. Additionally, the possibility of corrupt leaders overseeing resources and sustaining social cohesion could have brought the slow demise of these societies, which would lead to the formation of new social organizations and the rise of centralized states (Childe, 1950).

The Role of Power and Wealth in the Emergence of Corruption

Often defined as the abuse of entrusted power for personal gain, corruption is a phenomenon profoundly ingrained in the power structures and wealth in most human societies. As the early egalitarian groups became more complex social hierarchies, their wealth accumulation and power-wielding bred corruption. Let us explore how the wealth and power of a few elite individuals and groups contributed to the emergence of corrupt practices by tracking corruption and its origins from early human societies to more formalized and complex states.

Social Hierarchies and Power

In early human societies, decisions were made collectively, and their leadership roles were fundamentally based on merit or consensus rather than status or wealth. It was inevitable that social hierarchies would gradually emerge when societies transformed from nomadic hunter-gatherer groups to settled agricultural communities. Some individuals or groups accumulated more resources than others during the development of agriculture around 10,000 BCE, which allowed them to produce surplus food (Diamond, 1997).

The early social hierarchies turned more complex when specific individuals or families accumulated more surplus resources and rose to influential positions of authority. They were leaders who often controlled the most abundant land or had full access to significant resources and began to lord over their communities. Having control and power over resources and communities laid the conditions for corruption to emerge as those leaders in authority could now manipulate resources, labor, distribution of produce, and decision-making processes for personal gain (Service, 1975).

The abuse of power and control was aggravated by the fact that the leaders in many early societies were responsible for maintaining agricultural production, managing resources, and adjudicating disputes in communities. This situation supposes that the centralization of these public roles meant that the few individuals with authority had considerable influence, if not more control, over the lives of others. Such authority could be either used to help or abused to practice favoritism, nepotism, and other exploitative activities over subordinates. Authorities might tend to allocate abundant land to their own families or demand more share of the agricultural products in some cases (Goody, 1976).

The Accumulation of Wealth and Economic Inequalities

As wealth accumulation increased in the early societies, economic inequalities emerged. The accumulation of a surplus of resources is closely linked to the emergence of corruption, as wealth and control of resources often grant power and influence over social and political matters. The major determinant of social status in early agrarian societies is the capability to control land, livestock, and all other livelihood resources. In this case, wealthy individuals or groups with accumulated resources are very influential and could manipulate the economic and social processes for their own personal benefit (Childe, 1950).

The scenario created economic inequalities, which heightened cases of corruption. The wealthy could use their resources to sway leaders, secure exceptions, gain special treatment, or even bypass legal and social standards. These individuals or groups could bribe officials to reduce tax or, worse, be exempted from tax obligations, secure advantageous trade deals, or gain access to valuable resources. These corrupt activities blatantly subvert the fairness and integrity of the broader social system that sustains cohesion in the state (Graeber, 2011).

As societies grew more elaborate in this period, the function of wealth in corruption became even more evident. Wealth was closely linked to political power in Mesopotamia, Egypt, the Indus Valley, and other ancient civilizations. The elites could control the administrative and legal systems to their benefit. Such unfair advantages were often achieved through bribery, embezzlement, and other forms of corrupt behavior as officials sought to enrich themselves (Kenoyer, 1998).

In addition, wealthy individuals or groups started a corrupt patron-client practice, a form of relationship that is achieved by providing protection, favors, or financial support in exchange for loyalty and support services whenever or wherever demanded. As patrons used their wealth and influence to secure the loyalty of a client, this relationship would reinforce inequalities in social hierarchies and heighten corruption profoundly. Such a relationship could concoct a dependency and exploitation cycle, or symbioses, where the wealthy and powerful systematically continued to control and extract resources from the less powerful (Scott, 1972).

Power, Wealth, and Corruption in Early States

The play of the relationship between power, wealth, and corruption had its turning point during the emergence of early states. As states progressed and became more complex and centralized, it was coupled with worsening corruption. The accumulation of wealth obtained as gifts, tributes, taxation, and trade expansion in the hands of the ruling elite, who held the centralized power, would provide an abundant ground for corrupt practices.

The rulers and their officials in ancient states, such as those in Mesopotamia and Egypt, had extensive control over resources, labor force, and governmental and legal systems. Those in control and power had opportunities for corruption, as they could manipulate the distribution of resources, impose unfair taxes, and exploit the labor force for personal gain. In ancient Egypt, for example, the officials responsible for tax collection and resource management were notorious for embezzlement and bribery, using their status for personal enrichment at the expense of the state (Brewer & Teeter, 1999).

The ruling elite accumulated much wealth, further exacerbating corruption and leading to a greater hierarchical society and economic inequality. The more the rich accumulated wealth, the more the rich became more influential in political and legal systems, further widening the fissure between the rich and those in need. The unscrupulous wealthy often used bribes to gain favorable legal rulings, obtain access to lucrative business prospects, or evade military service. The concentration of wealth and power in the hands of a few individuals or families created a self-reinforcing cycle of corruption, where those with resources could continue to exploit the system to their advantage (Service, 1975).

The Legacy of Power and Wealth in Corruption

The relationship between power, wealth, and corruption has endured throughout cultures and societies with similar patterns across periods and places. The centralization of power and wealth has persistently been the crucial factor in the ascent and perpetuation of corruption from ancient Mesopotamia and Egypt to the empires of Rome and China, among others. As leaders and elites of such ancient civilizations and empires accumulated, they manipulated the systems of governance, law, and economics to serve their interests at the expense of the broader population (Diamond, 1997), which eventually led to the decline or collapse of their societies.

The legacy of this relationship continues to be relevant in our contemporary debates and discussions of corruption. Despite the advances in governance and legal systems in modern countries and regions, leaders and elites still wrestle with the challenges of corruption posed by the accumulation of wealth and abuse of power.

Studying the origins of corruption in early societies provides insights and can aid us in understanding the dynamics of corruption and possible solutions to address it today.

2.2. Historical Perspectives on Morality and Ethics in Corruption

The concepts and systems of morality and ethics have been central to human societies for millennia and have influenced individual behavior, groups, institutions, and political and economic systems. Various cultures and societies have created moral codes and ethical frameworks to guide their behavior, conduct daily dealings, and maintain social order throughout history. They used these moral and ethical standards to judge and condemn corrupt practices regarded as violations of the accepted social behavior norms.

Let us explore historical perspectives on morality and ethics about corruption by examining how ancient and modern societies have understood and responded to the corrupt actions of individuals and institutions.

Ancient Civilizations and the Moral Condemnation of Corruption

Ancient civilizations considered corruption an existing problem and a symptom of moral deficiency. Some early societies have developed legal codes to address corruption issues in administrating equality or justice, such as the Code of Hammurabi in Mesopotamia, circa 1754 BCE.

The Code specifies extreme punishments for judges who accepted bribes or passed unjust judgments, reflecting the belief that such behaviors violated legal and moral principles. According to Roth (1997), the condemnation of corruption in this moral context was closely tied to the concept of justice, which was understood as critical to sustaining social harmony and stability.

Likewise, the concept of 'ma'at'—a term that encompasses truth, justice, and cosmic order—was at the heart of the moral and ethical framework of ancient

Egyptian society. Society expected that the pharaoh would uphold "ma'at" and that corrupt behaviors were seen as threats and violations of this divine order.

The "Tale of the Eloquent Peasant" in Egyptian texts highlights the moral disgust associated with corrupt practices, especially when the officials abuse their authority and power. This tale is about a poor farmer, the protagonist, who is wronged by a corrupt official and seeks justice from higher authorities. The story emphasizes the critical role of justice and the moral responsibility of leaders to protect vulnerable and powerless individuals or groups from exploitation (Bard, 2008).

In ancient China, Confucian tradition emphasizes morality and ethics in governance. The emphasis on this tradition is highlighted by Confucius (551–479 BCE), who advocated for a government led by virtuous rulers who governed, lived by example, and possessed moral integrity. In this context, corruption was treated as a failure of moral leadership and a betrayal of the trust and faith of the people entrusted to rulers. Confucian ethics emphasized that rulers who failed to embody the virtues of "ren" (benevolence) and "li" (proper conduct) were believed to lose the Mandate of Heaven, the divine right to rule (Loewe, 1999).

The Confucian moral framework has influenced Chinese political thought and behavior, accepting how corruption was perceived and resolved in subsequent dynasties for centuries.

Classical Philosophies and Ethical Critiques of Corruption

The classical civilizations of Rome and Greece similarly wrestled with corruption and morality issues. The Ancient Greek philosophers, such as Plato and Aristotle, provided us with insightful critiques of corrupt practices. They link corruption to broader concerns about governance, justice, and the moral character of individuals or groups.

In Plato's "Republic," he explained that a just society requires leaders who are just and free from corruption themselves. Plato argued philosophically that the moral decay of rulers would bring down the state as corrupt rulers prioritize their own interests over the common good of the citizens (Plato, 2007).

In his 'Politics,' Aristotle also denounced corrupt practices in the political world of people holding official roles. Exploring various forms of government, Aristotle argued that the best form of governance is one where leaders seek the common good of the people rather than their own greater benefit.

According to Aristotle, corruption appears when leaders deviate from ethical standards and abuse their power for personal advantage. Aristotle believed that corruption is not only a practical problem but also a moral failure that could lead to the degeneration and eventual collapse of the political system (Aristotle, 1998).

Particularly in the Roman Republic, corruption was a pervasive concern in the later years when electoral bribery, patronage, and the concentration of wealth and power became widespread. Corruption, such as electoral bribery, patronage, and accumulation of wealth and power, worsened; thus, it was a pervasive concern, particularly in the later years of the Roman Republic.

Among famous Roman moralists, Cicero spoke out against corruption, linking it to the decline of civic virtues and the degeneration of the Roman Republic's political system that guided the institutions. Cicero's treatises emphasized the relevance of "virtus" (moral virtue) and "fides" (trustworthiness) in public life and denounced those who engaged in corrupt practice saying they betrayed the ideals of the Republic. Cicero also emphasized that corruption was not only a legal violation but also a moral disintegration endangering the stability and integrity of the Republic (Cicero, 2008).

Religious Perspectives on Corruption

Most ancient world religious traditions particularly shaped historical standpoints on corruption, as they framed it as a form of moral and spiritual degradation. For example, the Old and New Testaments in the Judeo-Christian tradition constantly condemn corruption. The Bible contains considerable passages denouncing corrupt behaviors such as those of judges and rulers.

For example, the book of Exodus (Exodus 23:8) commands, "You shall not take a bribe, for a bribe blinds the clear-sighted and subverts the cause of the just." This and more passages reflect the belief that corruption violates the divine law and betrays the moral and ethical responsibilities of leaders.

The New Testament clearly condemned corruption, particularly in the context of amassing wealth and abuse of power. Jesus Christ in the New Testament emphasizes the dangers of greed and the moral responsibility and accountability of the rich to act justly and charitably. The teaching of Jesus in the parable of the unjust steward (Luke 16:1-13) and other teachings highlight the ethical dimensions of financial and political conduct, which warn against the corrupting influence of money and the moral decay that can result from its pursuit of whatever it costs.

Islam, the closest religious tradition to Christianity, likewise condemns corruption as it violates moral and ethical principles. In addition, the Holy Quran explicitly addresses issues of justice, fairness, and the ethical behavior of leaders. The Quran provides numerous verses of warnings against bribery, fraud, and the abuse of power and authority.

A good example is in Surah Al-Baqarah (2:188), which states, "And do not consume one another's wealth unjustly or sent it [in bribery] to the rulers so that [they might aid] you [to] consume a portion of the wealth of the people in sin, while you know [it is unlawful]." This particular verse and more related verses reflect the Islamic view that corruption is a moral transgression that runs counter against social equality and the ethical order.

Medieval and Early Modern Perspectives

During the medieval and early modern periods, corruption continued to be a significant concern, particularly in the context of the church and monarchy. In the medieval and early modern periods, corruption flourished and continued to be a serious concern, especially in the context of the church and monarchy.

The Catholic Church in medieval Europe wielded immense power and was besieged with corruption within the church, including 'Simony' (the selling of church offices) and the sale of indulgences. These practices were seen as profound moral failings that undermined the spiritual integrity of the church and led to widespread calls for reform. Led by figures such as Martin Luther, the Protestant Reformation was essentially a portion of the response to the corrupt practices, framing them as proof of the moral deterioration within the church (Luther, 2003).

Also, the rise of absolutist monarchies in Early Modern Europe brought new concerns regarding corruption and the abuse of power by leaders and influential institutions. Montesquieu and Rousseau, in the Enlightenment period, for example, critiqued the concentration of significant powers on a few ruling monarchs and the question of the worsening corrupt behaviors of the elites. Montesquieu and Rousseau argued for the crucial functions of checks and balances and the need for moral and ethical governance of the state.

Particularly, Rousseau emphasized his idea and understanding that corruption worsens social inequality and the loss of civic virtue. Rousseau demanded a return to less complex and more egalitarian forms of governance, which tend to advance moral integrity and reduce the possibilities for corrupt behaviors among the ruling elites and monarchs (Rousseau, 2002).

Throughout history, corruption has been universally condemned across different cultures and religions for violating moral and ethical standards and threatening societal stability and integrity. This historical perspective continues to inform contemporary debates, emphasizing the importance of morality and ethics in governance and public life.

References

Aristotle. (1998). *Politics. (C. D. C. Reeve, Trans.)*. Hackett Publishing Company.

Bard, K. A. (2008). *An Introduction to the Archaeology of Ancient Egypt*. Wiley-Blackwell.

Brewer, D. J., & Teeter, E. (1999). *Egypt and the Egyptians*. Cambridge University Press.

Childe, V. G. (1950). *The Urban Revolution*. Town Planning Review, 21(1), 3-17.

Cicero, M. T. (2008). *On the Republic / On the Laws. (C. E. W. Steel, Ed.)*. Oxford University Press.

Diamond, J. (1997). *Guns, Germs, and Steel: The Fates of Human Societies*. W.W. Norton & Company.

Exodus 23:8. The Holy Bible. (2007). *English Standard Version*. Crossway.

Goody, J. (1976). *Production and Reproduction: A Comparative Study of the Domestic Domain*. Cambridge University Press.

Graeber, D. (2011). *Debt: The First 5,000 Years*. Melville House.

Kenoyer, J. M. (1998). *Ancient Cities of the Indus Valley Civilization*. Oxford University Press.

Loewe, M. (1999). *The Cambridge History of Ancient China: From the Origins of Civilization to 221 BC*. Cambridge University Press.

Luther, M. (2003). *Martin Luther's Basic Theological Writings*. Fortress Press.

Plato. (2007). *The Republic. (R. Waterfield, Trans.)*. Oxford University Press.

Quran 2:188. (2004). *The Holy Quran. (M. A. S. Abdel Haleem, Trans.)*. Oxford University Press.

Roth, M. T. (1997). *Law Collections from Mesopotamia and Asia Minor*. Scholars Press.

Rousseau, J.-J. (2002). *The Social Contract and The First and Second Discourses*. Yale University Press.

Scott, J. C. (1972). Patron-Client Politics and Political Change in Southeast Asia. *The American Political Science Review, 66*(1), 91–113.

Service, E. R. (1975). *Origins of the State and Civilization: The Process of Cultural Evolution*. W.W. Norton & Company.

CHAPTER 3.

CORRUPTION IN ANCIENT CIVILIZATIONS

3.1. Mesopotamia: Corruption and the Birth of Bureaucracy

Referred to as the "cradle of civilization," Mesopotamia (modern-day Iraq but historically including Iran, Turkey, Syria, and Kuwait) was home to some of the greatest cities and complex societies earlier in history. Mesopotamia, located between the Tigris and Euphrates rivers, consisted of the powerful city-states of Uruk, Ur, and Babylon, known in the ancient world to have laid the foundations for the ascent of writing, law, and administration. The necessity for structured governance and bureaucratic systems grew as these societies grew.

However, the nascent bureaucratic systems inevitably paid the price when corruption emerged. More discussions were held on how the early bureaucratic systems of Mesopotamia gave rise to corruption and its impacts on the governance, economy, and hierarchical societies of these ancient civilizations.

The Birth of Bureaucracy

The development of bureaucracy in Mesopotamia was their logical solution to management challenges posed by the vast urban population and their complicated economies. Rulers of the expanding city-states faced increasing challenges in governing various aspects, prompting them to delegate specific powers to various officials and administrators to help resolve the issues. These officials managed relatively essential roles such as tax collection, administration of justice, management of temples, and overseeing large-scale agricultural projects (Postgate, 1992).

The development of the writing system, such as the cuneiform script, played a crucial role in the growth of bureaucratic governance. Writing systems facilitated recording business transactions, legal codes, and administrative orders, providing a method for standardizing and enforcing governance across the burgeoning city-states. The ancient and known legal codes, including the Code of Ur-Nammu and the famous Code of Hammurabi, describe the early form of regulating society by Mesopotamian rulers employing written rules and decrees (Charpin, 2010).

However, the concentration of power and resources in the hands of bureaucrats and officials created opportunities for corruption. Contrary to their expected plan results, the systems they designed to manage and distribute resources quickly became channels for influential individuals to exploit their positions for personal benefit. The corrupt practices manifested in various forms, including embezzlement, bribery, and the manipulation of legal processes of the political system.

Corruption in the Administration of Justice

In Mesopotamia, administering justice was the most vulnerable field to corruption. Ironically, the judges and legal officials contradicted their roles in upholding laws and passing fair judgments as they were the main culprits of various forms of bribery and favoritism. Dating back to around 1754 BCE, the Code of Hammurabi explicitly acknowledges the existence of corrupt practices within the judicial system. The Code prescribes severe punishments for legal officials guilty of bribery and unjust verdicts (Roth, 1997).

However, corruption in ancient Mesopotamia persisted despite the legal safeguards and stricter prescribed rules. The Code of Hammurabi did not deter the continuation of corruption issues, as wealthy and influential individuals or families offered gifts or payments to judges and officials to sway the outcomes of legal disputes.

These corrupt practices eroded the public trust in the government and its ability to administer justice, aside from undermining the integrity of the legal system. The prevailing judicial corruption often contributed to and worsened social inequality. The rich could manipulate the legal system to their advantage while pushing away the poor and powerless with little or no alternatives.

Taxation and Economic Corruption

The complex economy of the city-states relied heavily on the collections from taxes in the form of agricultural produce, livestock, and labor. Even in the modern world, corruption in taxation still exists as it did in Mesopotamia. The sophisticated economy of the Mesopotamian city-states heavily relied on collecting taxes from diverse forms of labor, agrarian products, and livestock.

Usually elected from among the local elites and possessed significant influence, tax collectors frequently abused their position to overstate the amount owed and personally pocket the excess. Some tax collectors also accepted bribes from wealthy landowners in return for relieving their tax burdens, thus diverting the financial burden to the laborers and poorer farmers (Oates, 2004).

The impacts of corruption in tax collection were devastating to the economy of Mesopotamia. One of the major consequences is the incapacity of the government to fund public projects, such as the maintenance of vital irrigation systems, as the resources from the state are diverted to private hands. The manipulation of tax records and tax evasion practices caused resource shortages, social turmoil, and economic decline, aggravating financial inequalities and destabilizing city-states.

Religious Corruption in Temple Management

Religion played a central role in Mesopotamian society, with temples acting not only as places of worship but also as economic and administrative centers. In Mesopotamian society, religion played a significant role. Religious temples functioned as both worship and as economic and administrative centers.

The priests and religious officials in charge of the temples managed vast wealth, such as land, livestock, and labor. The concentration of wealth in the temple administration was a venue for the temptation to take advantage of opportunities. Priests and temple officials were often charged with embezzling religious offerings and stealing temple funds for their personal use.

The wealth and influence of these religious officials made them powerful political machineries whose corruption had tremendous impacts on the governance of the city-states. Corrupt temple officials tended to use their authority to sway political decisions that blurred the lines between religious and secular authority (Postgate, 1992).

The convergence of religious and economic power also ushered in the exploitation of the populace in Mesopotamia. The temple officials abused worshippers by making the sale of religious services more lucrative business, such as the granting of blessings or interpreting omens. The over-commercialization of religious practices degraded the spiritual substance of these rituals, which heavily placed additional financial burdens on ordinary people, who were frequently forced into making sacrificial offerings to ensure divine favor (Oates, 2004).

The Impact of Corruption on Mesopotamian Society

The rampant corruption in Mesopotamian society had a resounding consequence on the stability and longevity of its city-states. Despite the advanced bureaucratic systems that Mesopotamia designed, the system reveals its weakness as it is infiltrated with corruption, contributing to social and economic inequalities.

The concentration of wealth and power in the hands of corrupt elites brought them to social tensions and, in some cases, revolts against wealthy leaders, which led to society's eventual collapse. The decline of trust in legal institutions and the government weakened the social cohesion vital for city-states to function and be sustainable.

Corruption aggravated the issues posed by external threats, including aggression by neighboring peoples and internal strife, such as squabbles over a succession of authority and power. This incapacity to effectively address and curb corruption ultimately led to the decline and eventual collapse of the

Mesopotamian city-state civilizations (Charpin, 2010).

The experience of Mesopotamia on governance challenges reveals the advantages of establishing bureaucratic legal systems to manage urban governance issues. Ironically, the rise of these systems opened doors to corruption, which negatively impacted justice, taxation, and religious institutions. The corruption practices shown above are early examples of how governance effectiveness can contribute to the decline of advanced civilizations despite the existence of written laws and codes. More integrity systems must be developed and established to curb corruption and integrity issues during that period.

3.2. The Rise of City-States

Urbanization and governance, leading to the emergence of city-states such as Uruk, Ur, and Babylon (around 3500 BCE), indicates a consequential shift in human society by establishing governmental structures and systems. The condition for organized bureaucracies was more prominent as these city-states developed. In this section, we will explore the centralized control of resources and wealth, as well as the corrupt practices of officials who supervised the distribution of goods, tax collection, and legal matters in these early urban centers.

Furthermore, the centralization of control by the ruling elites and the appointed officials to control trade routes, agricultural surplus, and labor led to corrupt practices. This centralization often led the elites and officials to skim off the top of collected taxes or manipulate trade. These corrupt practices by government officials in the city of Uruk were especially implied in the famous Epic of Gilgamesh.

Temple Economies

The temples in Mesopotamian city-states were not only religious but also economic and administrative hubs. Priests have significant power, including managing land, labor forces, and stores of goods, which sometimes led to temptations of corruption and accusations of embezzlement and favoritism.

The system of sacrificial offerings to the gods was susceptible to abuse, with priests exploiting the religious devotion of the people for personal gain. This section explores evidence of such practices, blurring the lines between religious duty and personal enrichment.

Ancient Egypt: The Pharaonic Administration and Bribery

Ancient Egypt is one of the longest civilizations and is renowned for its monumental architecture, advanced agricultural methods, complex religious beliefs, arts, and sciences. The secret to the success and endurance of this civilization centered on its organized and hierarchical administration led by the pharaoh, who was regarded as a king and god.

The Pharaonic government oversaw everything, including tax collection, justice administration, and the construction of gigantic state projects like the pyramids. However, the complex and enormous demands to govern the massive projects in the hands of the pharaoh alone created opportunities for bribery, in particular. Below, we will explore how bribery has become pervasive at all levels of the Egyptian bureaucracy.

Structure and Responsibilities of the Pharaonic Administration

The complex and highly centralized system of the pharaonic administration was designed to manage vast resources and the various people of Egypt. The pharaoh, responsible for maintaining "*ma'at*" or cosmic order, was at the top of this hierarchy and seen as a divine ruler. Under the pharaoh were officials, including *viziers* (the highest official serving the pharaoh), provincial governors (nomarchs), and *scribes*, who were tasked with the daily administration of the state. These administrators managed the tax collection, agricultural resources, execution of public works, and the enforcement of laws (Brewer & Teeter, 1999).

The vizier, the right-hand man of the pharaoh, was the highest-ranking official who oversaw all aspects of government. Under the vizier were the nomarchs who managed the provinces or *nomes*, each with its local administration.

The scribes played a crucial role in the functioning of the administration. They kept records of everything, including land ownership, tax collections, legal proceedings, and other vital information. The integrity and competence of these officials were the backbone of the efficiency and stability of the Egyptian state.

Bribery in the Pharaonic Administration

The sophisticated pharaonic administration structure gave birth to the outstanding and beautiful achievements of the state. However, the centralization of power and resources in the hands of officials created opportunities for corruption. Bribery, in particular, became a normal practice in tax collection, legal administration, public works, and various governance features. The administration of justice was one of the most prevalent areas of bribery issues.

Egyptian society strongly emphasized law and order, and the pharaoh was seen as the ultimate judge who upheld *ma 'at*. Unfortunately, the judicial system was permanently tarnished by corrupt practices. The judges and legal officials were frequently susceptible and culprits of bribery. These judges and legal officials received bribes as gifts or payment from the rich or those with friendly connections. This unfair practice usually influences the outcomes of legal disputes in favor of the wealthy gift giver. This corrupt practice undermined the fairness of the established legal system, which eventually eroded public trust in the administration's capacity to deliver justice (Redford, 2001).

The "Tale of the Eloquent Peasant," a Middle Kingdom story, is one of the documents citing the prevalence of bribery in the legal system of ancient Egypt. The Tale highlights the suffering of a poor farmer who sought justice for being unjustly treated by a corrupt official. The poor farmer was repeatedly turned down in his attempts to obtain a fair hearing, as bribes from the powerful and wealthy party unduly influenced the judges and officials. The story happily ended when the pharaoh intervened and justly provided fair treatment to a farmer's story, which tells the broader societal issues of corruption, and the challenges other poorer citizens encounter in obtaining justice (Bard, 2008).

Taxes in ancient Egypt were collected from agricultural products, labor, and goods. The collections subsidized the construction of public infrastructure and supporting religious institutions. Known as 'scribes' or overseers, these tax collectors exerted considerable authority in their communities. The combined official power and lack of adequate oversight of the tax collectors led to the abuse of their authority. Some would inflate tax assessments and demand additional payments from the taxpayers, then pocket the difference for themselves.

Inequality in paying taxes also occurs when wealthy landowners bribe tax collectors to reduce their tax burdens. Due to this corrupt practice, the poorer farmers, laborers, and ordinary citizens suffer more financial burdens. This shift of financial responsibility and unfair practice aggravated both the economic imbalance and weakened the state's ability to collect sufficient revenue to finance its public service operations and sustain support to the citizens (Brewer & Teeter, 1999).

The construction of monumental projects and other public works, such as temples and pyramids, were other areas where bribery was widespread.

These massive projects require a significant labor force, finance, and resources, usually managed by high-ranking officials. These officials were tasked with ensuring the procurement of suitable quality materials, managing the labor adequately, and completing the projects on schedule.

Unfortunately, such immense-scale projects requiring vast wealth breed an opportunity for abuse of authority and corruption. The officials overseeing these projects accept bribes from contractors and suppliers in exchange for contracting awards or other beneficial favors to ignore the substandard construction materials they provide. This corrupt practice not only compromised the quality and safety of the structures but also increased the costs to the state (Redford, 2001).

The Impact of Bribery on Egyptian Society

The pervasiveness of bribery practically deteriorated the efficiency of the pharaonic administration. Corruption has diverted the resources of the state, thus reducing its capability to fund essential services, sustain the infrastructure, and support more public projects. The corrupt environment weakened the overall stability of ancient Egypt, making it more vulnerable to internal turmoil and external threats.

Bribery also worsened the issue of social inequality in ancient Egypt. The rich can influence the decisions of the officials on various matters that worsen the division between the elites and the ordinary people. The rich could manipulate the legal system to their benefit, while the poor and ordinary citizens were on the losing side, with no access to justice and fair treatment. This social inequality produced social tensions and also undermined the legitimacy of the pharaonic administration that was established and supposed to pursue the principle of '*ma'at*' or cosmic order and justice (Bard, 2008).

Corruption within the administration eroded the moral authority of the pharaoh and his officials. Obeyed and respected as a divine ruler, the pharaoh was responsible for preserving harmony and order in the kingdom. Unfortunately, corruption and bribery starkly opposed this idea, which led to cynicism and disillusionment among the people. The erosion of trust in the ability of the government to uphold justice and order worsened social unrest and economic instability, leading to the eventual collapse of the Old and Middle Kingdoms (Redford, 2001).

Efforts to Combat Bribery and Corruption

Before the eventual collapse of ancient Egypt due to the pervasive nature of corruption, there were efforts and attempts to curb corruption and restore the integrity of the pharaonic rule.

During the reign of Pharaoh Horemheb (c. 1319–1292 BCE), for example, a series of edicts were promulgated to reduce the abuse of authority and power by entrusted officials. These edicts are inscribed on 'stelae (stone slabs or columns), which included measures to punish corrupt officials and protect the rights of ordinary citizens. Pharaoh Horembeb's reform efforts demonstrate the destructive impact of corruption, especially bribery, on the state and concerted efforts to regain justice and order in society (Brewer & Teeter, 1999).

Also, during the reign of Pharaoh Senusret III (c. 1878–1839 BCE) in the Middle Kingdom, he implemented reforms to limit the power of the 'nomarchs' and centralizing authority. Partially, these reforms motivated the need to reduce the rampant corrupt practices and abuses in the provinces.

The reforms were able to reduce the autonomy of the nomarchs and increase the oversight of local officials, which helped Senusret III restore the integrity of the administration and ensure the state functioned again efficiently (Bard, 2008).

In sum, bribery was a major challenge for the pharaonic administration in ancient Egypt as it permeated various levels of governance and affected everything, including the administration of justice, tax collection, and public works. Despite efforts to combat bribery, its persistence contributed to social inequality, economic instability, and the eventual decline of the Old and Middle Kingdoms. The experience of ancient Egypt is a reminder of the challenges of sustaining a just and effective government that still stands and confronts the present governments around the world today.

3.3. Indus Valley Civilization: Speculative Corruption and Economic Inequities

The Indus Valley Civilization, also known as the Harappan Civilization, flourished between approximately 3300 BCE and 1300 BCE in what is now modern-day Pakistan and northwest India. Known as the Harappan Civilization, the Indus Valley Civilization emerged approximately between 3300 BCE and 1300 BCE. Located in modern-day Pakistan and northwest India, the Harappan Civilization is one of the earliest known urban cultures contemporaneous with ancient Egypt and Mesopotamia.

However, the sophistication of the Indus Valley Civilization's planning, social structure, and trade networks remain shrouded in mystery fundamentally due to the undeciphered script, which needed much study to unravel how that civilization functioned.

Some speculations about the civilization based on archaeological evidence and comparisons with other ancient civilizations state that there was a presence of corruption and economic inequalities within the Indus Valley Civilization. Such integrity issues and other unfavorable elements have shaped the society, and their behavior contributed to its eventual decline and collapse.

Urban Planning and Social Hierarchies

Harappa, Mohenjo-Daro, and Dholavira were the cities of the Indus Valley civilization that were remarkable for their advanced urban planning. These cities featured grid-pattern streets, sophisticated drainage systems, and giant public buildings, suggesting a highly organized and centralized planned society. This infrastructure indicates a complex administrative system involving only a hierarchy of officials responsible for various management features, including water distribution, waste removal, trade regulation, and legal system (Kenoyer, 1998).

That bureaucratic system implies the potential and opportunity for corruption, as observed in other civilizations where authority and resources are in the hands of only powerful bureaucrats and rulers. We can only speculate that officials and elites may have engaged in embezzlement or favoritism as in charge of the distribution of goods, allocation of labor, and overseers of construction projects due to a lack of recorded or written materials.

Economic Inequalities in the Indus Valley Civilization

Despite the lack of archaeological evidence, some discoveries suggest that wealth and resources needed to be adequately distributed among the population. The existence of larger and properly built houses among smaller and modest dwellings indicates a degree of social stratification.

Findings suggest that larger houses uncovered in the citadel areas of Mohenjo-Daro and other cities may have been the domiciles of the administrators, merchants, or priests who managed significant economic and political positions and such elite class. In contrast, the smaller and simpler houses in the lower city could be the domiciles of laboring classes, including artisans, farmers, and workers who were the usual subject to the authority of the elites (Possehl, 2002).

The social stratification portrayed by the sizes and locations of houses suggests the existence of economic inequalities, which were aggravated by corruption within the administrative systems. If the elite authorities could manipulate the allocation of resources and labor to their benefit, it could have created a society where wealth and privilege were consolidated among a small group in the population. At the same time, the most significant members lived under uncomplicated living conditions.

The extensive trade networks that connected the Indus Valley with Mesopotamia, Central Asia, and the Persian Gulf would provide better opportunities for the wealthy elites to double their wealth. Kenoyer (1998) thought merchants and traders were part of the elites who may have engaged in corrupt practices such as hoarding goods, manipulating prices, or forming monopolies that further entrenched economic inequalities.

Speculative Corruption in Trade and Governance

The most critical aspect of the economic prosperity of the Indus Valley Civilization was its extensive trade networks. Its cities were central to its commerce, dealing with various goods such as cotton textiles, beads, pottery, and metalwork, which were traded within the region and outside with distant territories. The control of these trade networks was likely a significant source of wealth and power as those in positions of authority could exploit it for personal gain.

As implied by the urban planning and extensive trade network in a society with a sophisticated bureaucracy, corruption could have resulted in officials demanding bribes in exchange for favorable trade terms or manipulating trade routes to benefit favored merchants or regions. In this scenario, such practices could have led to wealth accumulation among a small elite of influential individuals or families, leaving most of the population to reap meager or no benefits from the thriving trade (Possehl, 2002).

Furthermore, the construction and maintenance of the advanced drainage and water management systems, among other public works administration, would have required more significant labor and resources to be implemented and accomplished. The allocation of labor for public works could have facilitated corrupt officials to thrive by demanding bribes or favors to allot less tedious tasks or even to exempt favored individuals from labor duties altogether. Wright (2010) indicated that such corrupt practices have placed tremendous burdens on the lower classes, aggravating economic inequalities and potentially leading to social turmoil.

The Decline of the Indus Valley Civilization

Scholars have debated the collapse of the Indus Valley Civilization that flourished around 1900 BCE. Climate change, the drying up of the Ghaggar-Hakra River, invasions, and internal decline due to social and economic factors are some of the theories proposed to explain the decline of the civilization. Despite the unclear causes of the collapse of civilization, some scholars conjectured that internal corruption and the resulting economic inequalities could have contributed to the downfall of the Indus Valley Civilization.

Similar to other ancient civilizations, corruption within the administration could have debilitated the state to respond to external and internal challenges. The accumulation and concentration of resources and power in the hands of a corrupt elite might have led to social tensions, which loosened the cohesion and resilience of the whole civilization against challenges. In addition, the mismanagement of resources and trade and the exploitation of the ordinary working classes could have undermined the economic foundation, posing greater vulnerability to environmental changes and external threats to civilization (Wright, 2010).

In short, the Indus Valley Civilization was a highly organized society with a complex bureaucracy, a system that ironically likely led to corruption, economic inequalities, and social stratification. These factors may have contributed to the decline of the civilization, offering us valuable insights into how corruption and inequality can undermine advanced societies.

3.4. China's Dynasties: The Mandate of Heaven and Moral Decay

Central to understanding the political and moral philosophy that shaped the governance of ancient China is the concept of the "Mandate of Heaven." The Mandate of Heaven was a divine right to rule, granted by heaven to the emperor (or dynasty) who governed with virtue and righteousness and emerged during the Zhou Dynasty in 1046-256 BCE.

However, the rebellion and the rise of a new ruling house justified their actions when they did not heed the Mandate, believing that a dynasty or emperor suffered corruption and moral decay. The cycle of dynastic rise and fall throughout Chinese history was often described in terms of the Mandate of Heaven, claiming that corruption played a crucial role in the moral and political decline that precipitated the collapse of dynasties.

Let us explore how corruption and moral decay in the Chinese imperial court and bureaucracy led to the deterioration of the Mandate of Heaven, contributing to the fall of China's prominent dynasties.

The Mandate of Heaven: Governance and Moral Order

The Mandate of Heaven was a moral and political doctrine that required the emperor, the "Son of Heaven," to rule with benevolence and justice and follow Confucian principles. The emperor responsible for sustaining harmony in the empire was seen as the intermediary between heaven and earth.

If the state and society are stable and the people prosper, they are manifestations that the emperor has governed well and under the Mandate. However, the Mandate could be withdrawn if the emperor and his administration became corrupt, oppressive, or morally bankrupt and when social unrest, disasters, and other signs of divine disapproval occurred (Feng, 2011).

Therefore, the legitimacy of a dynasty is understood through its ability to uphold moral integrity and productive governance. This mindset was deeply ingrained in the Chinese political fabric and used as the standard to justify the rise and fall of dynasties. Thus, corruption was understood not only as a practical problem but also as a moral failing with potentially cosmic consequences.

Corruption in the Zhou Dynasty: The Origins of the Mandate of Heaven

The Zhou Dynasty overthrew the Shang Dynasty and is credited with formulating the belief of the Mandate of Heaven to legitimize their existence to govern the empire. The Zhou rulers believed the Shang lost the Mandate of Heaven because of their corrupt practices and tyrannical behavior, especially under Zhou Xi, the last Shang king.

Based on the accounts, King Zhou Xi was a despot who indulged in excessive luxury while allowing his court to be corrupt and ignoring the poor circumstances of his people. Zhou Xi's failure to govern with equality and moral impairment caused the loss of divine favor, leading to the subsequent victory of the Zhou Dynasty (Loewe, 1999).

During the early days of their rule, the kings of the Zhou dynasty were initially praised for their virtuous rule and the establishment of a moral order based on Confucian ethics. However, the positive views and praises faded when corruption started seeping into the administration as the dynasty expanded. The Eastern Zhou (770-256 BCE) of the later Zhou period was marked by political fragmentation as their local feudal princes (local lords) accumulated more power at the expense of the central authority.

These local lords engaged themselves in exploiting peasants, bribery, nepotism, and other corrupt practices, weakening the ability of the state to govern effectively. Due to moral decay and political fragmentation, the Zhou Dynasty declined, and the Warring States period rose, leading to chaos and setting the opportune ground for the emergence of the Qin Dynasty (Loewe, 1999).

The Qin Dynasty: Legalism and Corruption

The Qin Dynasty (221–206 BCE), despite its short duration, was a pivotal period in Chinese history. Qin Shi Huang, the first emperor of China, implemented a centralized and authoritarian system of government based on Legalist principles. The Qin Dynasty (221-206 BCE) was a pivotal period in Chinese history despite its short span. The first emperor of China, Qin Shi Huang, established a centralized and authoritarian rule based on Legalist principles.

This legalism emphasized stringent laws, harsh punishments, and the absolute authority of the state. This authoritarian system has supported Qin Shi Huang to unify China. However, the system ironically fostered an environment where corruption could thrive, especially among officials who wielded unhinged power. With all power flowing directly from the emperor, the bureaucracy was turned highly central during the Qin Dynasty period.

While this system effectively consolidated control over the entire land and resources, local officials exploited their positions despite the presence of local oversight. Tax collection and the administration of justice, among other corrupt practices, became rampant. The combined corrupt practices and harsh legal system have consistently driven widespread resentment among the populace (Lewis, 2007).

The empire suffered chaos, with revolts breaking across the country, swiftly and brutally leading to the downfall of the dynasty after the death of Qin Shi Huang. It is believed that the significant factors in the rebellion were the corruption and brutality of the Qin officials, ultimately leading to the collapse of the Qin Dynasty.

Lewis (2007) indicated that the failure of the Qin Dynasty to uphold the Mandate of Heaven, as evidenced by their inability to govern justly, causing widespread suffering of the populace, set the opportune stage for the rise of the Han Dynasty.

The Han Dynasty: The Mandate of Heaven and the Erosion of Power

Considered one of China's golden ages, the Han Dynasty (206 BCE-220 CE) is characterized by an extended period of stability, socio-cultural posterity, and economic development. The adoption of Confucianism as the state ideology by the Han emperors was instrumental in sustaining the stability of the state for an extended period. However, despite the emphasis on moral integrity, justice, and good governance, corruption seeped through the administration, particularly eroding the integrity of the imperial court.

During the Han Dynasty period, the influence of eunuchs in the imperial court was one of the most notorious forms of corrupt practices. Eunuchs were close attendants to the emperor and used that status to wield considerable power behind the scenes. During their service, many eunuchs became corrupt, abusing their influence to manipulate court politics and enrich themselves. Most of them formed factions, engaged in bribery, and at times orchestrated the removal of officials who disagreed with them. Such corrupt practices led to mistrust in the imperial administration, which contributed to the erosion of central authority (Twitchett & Loewe, 1986).

The Han Dynasty culminated its decline in the Wang Mang interregnum (9–23

CE), as it seized the throne and attempted to implement radical reforms. Despite Wang Mang's aim to resolve economic inequalities and curb corruption, the attempts were poorly implemented and met with resistance from the influential elites. Wang Mang failed to restore order which was seen as an indication that he lost the Mandate of Heaven. He was overthrown, and the Han Dynasty was restored, known as the Later Han Dynasty (Twitchett & Loewe, 1986).

The Later Han, however, continued to suffer from corruption and internal decay. Despite its restoration efforts, the Later Han suffered from corruption and internal turmoil. The local warlords kept misusing their power, the officials continued practicing corruption, and the eunuchs and the empresses' families manipulated the imperial court. The moral decay and political instability of the Later Han eventually fragmented the empire into the Three Kingdoms, marking the end of the Han Dynasty (Lewis, 2007).

Summing up, the Mandate of Heaven was a powerful ideological force that influenced the rise and fall of dynasties in ancient China. The Mandate underpinned the moral obligation of the emperor to govern justly and uphold social harmony. However, historical records reveal that corruption and moral decay within the imperial court resulted in the loss of the integrity of the Mandate.

The overthrow of the corrupt Shang by the Zhou Dynasty and the rapid decline of the brutal Qin Dynasty led to the decline of the Han Dynasty. The Mandate of Heaven served as a guiding principle and a cautionary tale but failed when challenged and faced with corruption issues and internal conflicts of the dynasty. The repetitive pattern of dynastic rise and fall highlights the perils of corruption and the significance of upholding moral integrity in governance. These lessons remain relevant in our contemporary political discourse.

References

Bard, K. A. (2008). *An Introduction to the Archaeology of Ancient Egypt*. Wiley-Blackwell.

Brewer, D. J., & Teeter, E. (1999). *Egypt and the Egyptians*. Cambridge University Press.

Charpin, D. (2010). *Writing, Law, and Kingship in Old Babylonian Mesopotamia.* University of Chicago Press.

Feng, L. (2011). *Early China: A Social and Cultural History.* Cambridge University Press.

Kenoyer, J. M. (1998). *Ancient Cities of the Indus Valley Civilization.* Oxford University Press.

Lewis, M. E. (2007). *The Early Chinese Empires: Qin and Han.* Harvard University Press.

Loewe, M. (1999). *The Cambridge History of Ancient China: From the Origins of Civilization to 221 BC.* Cambridge University Press.

Oates, J. (2004). Babylon. Thames & Hudson.

Possehl, G. L. (2002). *The Indus Civilization: A Contemporary Perspective.* Rowman Altamira.

Postgate, J. N. (1992). *Early Mesopotamia: Society and Economy at the Dawn of History.* Routledge.

Redford, D. B. (2001). *The Oxford Encyclopedia of Ancient Egypt.* Oxford University Press.

Roth, M. T. (1997). *Law Collections from Mesopotamia and Asia Minor.* Scholars Press.

Twitchett, D., & Loewe, M. (1986). *The Cambridge History of China: Volume 1, The Ch'in and Han Empires, 221 BC–AD 220.* Cambridge University Press.

Wright, R. P. (2010). *The Ancient Indus: Urbanism, Economy, and Society.* Cambridge University Press.

CHAPTER 4.

CORRUPTION IN CLASSICAL CIVILIZATIONS

4.1. Introduction

It is known that the most influential societies recorded in history are the classical civilizations of Greece, Rome (Italy), the Maurya Empire, and the Achaemenid Empire. Our modern time owed so much to these civilizations that made sacrifices and laid the groundwork for our modern governance, philosophical thoughts, legal systems, and deeper cultural understanding. However, similar to the societies that preceded them, these societies suffered the brunt of corruption, which brought them to their eventual decline. Let us explore how corruption manifested in various ways and depths, which affected the political systems, economies, and social stratification of these greatest classical societies.

Ancient Greece was the birthplace of democracy, a thought we are attempting to practice for the last centuries. However, despite its advanced political systems, corruption relentlessly emerged as the greatest threat to the integrity of its political institutions. Athens, the capital of Greece, is particularly known for its application of democratic approaches to governance and for confronting challenges in sustaining leadership and political transparency and accountability. The capital revealed the vulnerabilities inherent in their advanced governance system, such as rampant bribery, electoral manipulation, and the misuse of public funds. Athens and other great Green city-states eventually declined as varied corrupt practices corroded the democratic ideals they tried to realize.

Democracy, Republics, and the Corruption of Power

As pillars of Western political thought, the classical civilizations of Greece and Rome introduced concepts like democracy, republicanism, and the rule of law. These two famous civilizations worked hard to advance their concepts but still suffered severe corruption, which debilitated their governance system and led to their decline as advanced societies.

Corruption manifested in forms such as bribery, electoral manipulation, and the concentration of authority and power among the few elites in Athens and Rome. These particular corrupt practices were the primary negative elements that led to the erosion of public trust and the eventual collapse of their political structures.

Corruption in Athenian Democracy

Often celebrated as the birthplace of democracy, Athens provides a complex and revealing case study of how corruption can penetrate the most advanced and pioneering political systems. The Athenian model of democracy was designed to ensure broad participation and prevent concentration of power where citizens participated actively in decision-making. Despite that ideal model, it provided a fertile environment for corrupt practices. In particular, corruption in Athens occurred largely in public offices and the judicial system in the form of bribery.

Often chosen by lot, public officials were expected to serve the state with integrity, but the lack of robust enforcement transparency mechanisms allowed for widespread bribery. The corrupt practice of bribery was rampant among wealthy individuals and families and influential politicians who would bribe officials to secure favors and/or avoid prosecution. Such corruption even extended to popular courts where jurors could be bribed by gifts or promises of benefits and favors, which sabotaged the fairness of the judicial process and outcome (Finley, 1973).

Electoral corruption also infiltrated the Athenian democratic system. Public offices were filled by lot; however, particular positions were filled by elected personalities, such as generals (strategoi). These elections often became a competition of wealth rather than merit as candidates spend vast sums to secure their votes. The elites and oligarchs exploited powers to manipulate elections and political strategies that bolster their influence over political and material resources. These political malpractices impacted the democratic principles of Athens, which further contributed to the increasing division between the rich and the poor, as well as more social unrest and political turmoil (Ober, 1989).

A mechanism of ostracism was established intended to safeguard against the rise of tyrants. In spite of its good intentions and strengths, some elites were able to use the mechanism as a tool for political manipulation. The wealthy could influence the outcome of ostracism votes by bribing citizens or spreading fake accusations against their opponents. The abuse of ostracism manifested how the well-intentioned mechanisms could be corrupted, thus eroding trust in the democratic process.

Corruption in the Roman Republic

Lasting from 509 BCE to 27 BCE, the Roman Republic is also a suitable example demonstrating governance that ultimately succumbed to corruption and downfall. The Republic featured a complex system of checks and balances devised to prevent an individual from accumulating much power and authority. However, particularly the electoral system, the Senate, and the administration of the provinces turned corrupt and pervasive as Rome expanded its territories and accumulation of wealth.

During the later years of the Republic, electoral corruption in the Roman Republic was rampant. A common practice among candidates seeking public office became a system called "ambitus," or electoral bribery.

Spending vast sums of wealth to secure critical positions, such as consul or praetor, wealthy patricians, and ambitious politicians used their resources to buy votes. Ambitus, obviously, distorted the electoral process and led to the concentration of power only among the few wealthy elites, undermining the democratic ideals of the Roman Republic (Gruen, 1974).

Being regarded as the guardian of the stability and integrity of the Republic, the Senate was not immune to corruption. They were famous for abusing their positions to advance their personal or familial benefits rather than the state. As powerful senatorial families sought to maintain their influence, they resort to bribery, patronage, and manipulating legal processes. The unrepublican practices of corrupt senators were detrimental to the authority and integrity of the Senate, especially in terms of checks and balances of the Republic's institutions (Syme, 1939).

During the Roman Republic, provincial governance was another area where corruption was unbridled. The administration of the provinces became increasingly essential and lucrative as the Roman Empire expanded. The provinces were governed by governors, given significant autonomy over their provinces, and mainly were appointed from the senatorial class. With personal ambition for benefits, governors exploited their positions by engaging in extortion, embezzlement, and exploiting local populations. Due to the exploitative and ambitious activities of the governors, many provincial subjects of Rome became alienated, making people resentful, rebellious, and unwilling to provide resources to the Republic (Tacitus, 1999).

From Republic to Empire

The ascent and the collapse of the Roman Empire could be attributed to the widespread corruption in the Roman Republic. Ambitious leaders like Julius Caesar exploited the vulnerabilities of the Roman political system as the Republic suffered the impacts of corruption.

Caesar's accumulated power was facilitated by political maneuvering and support from the corrupt and disenfranchised populace. This event marked the beginning of the end of the Republic. The concentration of power in the hands of individuals and the erosion of traditional republican values set the environment for the emergence of imperial rule (Syme, 1939).

Corruption became institutionalized, and the imperial court became the center of intrigue, bribery, and patronage under the Roman Empire. The Empire achieved significant territorial and cultural accomplishments despite the corrupt practices that continued undermining its stability.

Eventually, the Western Roman Empire declined and fell in the 5th century CE, which can be attributed to the combined crippling impacts of the deep-seated corruption and its incapacity to government effectively and respond to external aggression.

Let it be known that the complex and valuable experiences of ancient Greece and Rome illustrate how corruption can sabotage political systems that were meant to sustain prosperous societies. However, they are the very systems exploited by corrupt leaders, leading to social and political instability and the collapse of structures. Corruption brought down the democratic and republican ideals, which underscore the importance of integrity and accountability in governance.

4.2. The Fall of the Roman Empire

The Roman Republic and the Empire are profound examples of how corruption can destabilize a strong state and eventually bring it into the depths of collapse. Notably, corruption became endemic in the Roman Republic as the state expanded and wealth accumulated only among the few elites.

The leaders crafted the electoral system of the Roman Republic to prevent the concentration of power on anyone. Despite the advanced strategies of the electoral system, the wealthy and influential elites uncovered its weaknesses and exploited them by buying influence and securing high positions. As corruption became systemic, Roman citizens lost their trust in the system, leading to the ascent of autocratic leaders who transitioned the Republic into the Roman Empire.

Corruption became institutionalized--bribery and patronage permeated all levels of government under the Empire. Let us examine how corruption in the transition from Republic to Empire has contributed to the eventual decline of the great Roman civilization.

The Roman Empire: Corruption and the Fall of Rome

The Roman Empire is one of the most powerful empires in history, but it declined and eventually fell in the 5th century CE. The fall of the Roman Empire was due to a complex and extended series of events aggravated by various contributing factors such as economic crises, military defeats, and internal strife. These numerous factors could be some of the fruits that corruption bred, which played a crucial role in the decline of the Empire.

Various forms of corruption seeped through Roman life, including the political, military, and economic aspects. Corruption sowed distrust in the government and the effectiveness of the military, which resulted in an unstable political system and started to diminish the economy.

Political Corruption and the Erosion of Integrity

Corruption became rampant during the later years in the political structure of the Roman Empire. The imperial office became the center of corruption, including the succession of emperors, which was determined by bribery, intrigue, and the manipulation of power rather than by merit or legal succession. These political practices at the highest levels of the government were the debilitating factors that sabotaged the legitimacy of the ruling class of the Empire.

The role of the Praetorian Guard, the elite unit responsible for the protection of the emperor, was one of the most significant manifestations of political corruption. Contrary to its original function, the Praetorian Guards became a powerful political force using its influence to make and unmake emperors. The Guards were engaged in the unlawful sale of the imperial throne, auctioning it to the highest bidder. This corruption was notoriously seen during the rule of the Five Emperors (193 CE) when the Praetorian Guard literally sold the Empire to Didius Julianus (Tacitus, 1999), which disrupted the succession process and eroded the authority of the emperor by reducing the office to a for-sale commodity.

Moreover, once the backbone of the Roman Republic and an advisory body to the emperor, the Senate became increasingly corrupt. Rather than the welfare of the Empire, most Senators were more concerned with their wealth and influence. Rather than merit, senatorial offices were often secured through financial incentives, rampant bribery, and favoritism. The degradation of the role of the Senate contributed to the deterioration of the checks and balances, which were the trademark of Roman governance (Syme, 1939).

Military Corruption and the Decline of Roman Power

The Roman military, which existed even long before the formidable institution, was not immune to corruption. The military became increasingly besieged by corruption issues, including the embezzlement of funds, the sale of military positions, and the degradation of discipline. These issues severely eroded the effectiveness of the war of the Roman legions, which were the backbone of the Roman conquest, expansion, and defense.

The major military corruption was committed by commanders and quartermasters who embezzled the money allocated for the salaries of the soldiers and their provisions. This corrupt practice deprived the troops of military supplies and due salaries, making them less motivated and effective to fight in battle. These factors made the military incapable, making the Empire weaker and powerless against external aggressions by Germanic tribes and the Huns, among other aggressors, which slowly overpowered the Western Roman Empire (Ostrogorsky, 1969).

In particular, during the later years of the Empire, the sale of military positions further exacerbated corrupt practices. Studies show that the wealthy and influential elites could buy command positions regardless of their experience or ability. This particular practice contributed to the decline in the quality of military leadership as these commanders were more interested in personal benefits than in the effective military power of the Empire. Such corrupt practices resulted in the loss of competent leadership, a crucial element in the military losses the Empire suffered in its final centuries (Treadgold, 1997).

Furthermore, corruption has increased due to the decline in discipline within the ranks of the Roman army. Often demoralized by poor pay and the lack of proper equipment, soldiers were more likely to engage in looting, desertion, and other forms of misconduct. The lack of discipline and demoralized soldiers further weakened the once formidable Roman legions to defend the borders and sustain the internal stability of the Empire.

Corruption and the Collapse of the Roman Economy

Corruption played a significant part in the economic crises and collapse of the Roman Empire. Tax evasion by the wealthy, the debasement of currency, and the exploitation of public resources for personal gain by incompetent officials sabotage the once robust and expansive economy of the Empire.

The evasion of taxes by the elite was one of the most debilitating forms of economic corruption. The influential rich landowners often used their connections with government officials to evade taxes, an illegal activity that shifted the tax burden onto the poorer citizens. This socially irresponsible practice led to a massive decline in state revenues, which hindered the military and public works of the Empire from functioning correctly. This corruption triggered economic decline, further setting social unrest and weakening the social fabric of the Empire (Ostrogorsky, 1969).

Another symptom of economic corruption in the Empire was the debasement of currency, where the government reduced the silver content of coins to stretch the finances of the Empire. This debasement led to rampant inflation and the devaluation of money and further destabilized the economy despite its short-term relief to the imperial treasury. The problems of poverty and inequality exacerbated by the resulting economic instability further contributed to the decline of the urban centers, formerly economic hubs of the Empire (Treadgold, 1997).

Moreover, corrupt officials often exploit public resources for personal gain. Governors and government officials embezzled public project funds for infrastructure maintenance and military supplies. Embezzlement deteriorated the capability of the Empire to sustain itself, led to the failure of essential services, and plunged the overall quality of life of Roman citizens (Tacitus, 1999).

The Impact of Corruption on the Fall of Rome

The incremental impact of political, military, and economic corruption was widespread for the Roman Empire. The impact of corruption on the effectiveness of the imperial institutions also undermined the trust and loyalty of its citizens. The disillusionment of the people with the corrupt and inept government led to low civic participation and a fragile social cohesion that once held the Empire together for a long period.

Corruption brought down essential social and political structures supporting Roman power when the Western Roman Empire collapsed in 476 CE. The Empire could not withstand the combined issues caused by internal decay and external pressures. Although corruption was not the sole cause of the collapse, it was the critical factor that accelerated the decline and made the Empire more vulnerable to its numerous crises.

The fall of the Roman Empire illustrates the devastating impact of corruption. Political, military, and economic corruption weakened the Empire's foundations, ultimately leading to its collapse. The story of the Roman Empire is a reminder of the importance of integrity and accountability in maintaining the strength and stability of any state.

4.3. The Maurya Empire

The Maurya Empire is one of ancient India's most powerful and extensive empires. The Empire was concerned about corruption, especially during the reign of Chandragupta Maurya and his advisor Kautilya (ISO: Cāṇakya, 375–283 BCE). 'Arthashastra,' a treatise on statecraft by Kautilya, provides us with one of the earliest comprehensive analyses of corruption with various details of how officials could abuse their positions for personal gain.

Let us explore the insights of Kautilya on corruption, the measures it proposed to combat corruption, and the extent to which these ideas were implemented in governing the Maurya Empire. Furthermore, we will explore how corruption impacted the administration of the Empire and how it contributed to its eventual decline.

The Maurya Empire: Kautilya's Arthashastra and State Corruption

The Maurya Empire (4th century BCE) is one of ancient India's most significant and influential empires. Under the administration of Chandragupta Maurya and his successors, the Empire expanded and encompassed vast lands stretching across the Indian subcontinent.

Administering such extensive territory requires a complex and sophisticated system of governance. That system was meticulously inscribed in the 'Arthashastra,' a treatise attributed to Kautilya (Chanakya), the chief advisor to Chandragupta Maurya.

The Arthashastra is one of the earliest and most comprehensive achievements on statecraft and political economy, with detailed insights into governance, military strategy, and the management of corruption within the state. Let us discuss how Kautilya's 'Arthashastra' addressed the state corruption issue and how these ideas were implemented in the governance of the Maurya Empire.

Kautilya's Arthashastra: An Overview

The Arthashastra covers a wide range of statecraft-related topics, including administration, law, economics, diplomacy, and warfare. Written in Sanskrit, this treatise is considered one of the most politically influential texts in ancient Indian political thought. The approach of Kautilya to governance is highly pragmatic, focusing on the effective use of resources and power to sustain the stability and prosperity of the state. The Arthashastra is primarily concerned with the practical aspects of ruling, including preventing and managing corruption, which is remarkably different from other ancient texts (Kangle, 1965).

Kautilya was cognizant of the dangers that corruption would bring to the administration. He understood that the concentration of power in the hands of a few influential government officials opens doors for corruption, which could sabotage the efficacy of governance and debilitate the state. Therefore, in the Arthashastra, Kautilya devoted significant attention to identifying the various manifestations of corruption and presented strategies to combat them. Katilya's priority actions on corruption reflect his understanding that a corrupt administration is nothing good but social unrest, economic decline, and the collapse of the state.

Forms of Corruption in the Maurya Empire

Kautilya identified various forms of corruption, most of which are still relevant in contemporary governance discussions. The Arthashastra identified embezzlement as one of the most significant forms of corruption, particularly among government officials trusted to manage state finances and resources. Kautilya famously describes the challenge of identifying embezzlement by comparing it to a fish swimming in water. Knowing whether a fish is drinking water or simply swimming is difficult. It is equally challenging to know whether an official is misappropriating funds (Kangle, 1965). The metaphor of the fish underscores the inherent challenges in monitoring corruption in a complex imperial administration.

Bribery is another form of corruption highlighted in the Arthashastra. In particular, government officials in positions of authority, such as judges, tax collectors, and military officers, were the easiest people to take bribes in return for favors or actions. Kautilya understood that bribery undermined the fairness of the legal and administrative systems and could erode public trust in the government. He recognized that the existence of corruption could lead to a deterioration in the rule of law, where only the wealthy could avail and afford to pay justice.

Kautilya was also significantly concerned in his analysis of corruption and the impacts of nepotism and favoritism. He cautioned the government against appointing officials based on personal influence or connections rather than merit, which could lead to inefficiency and the abuse of power. Kautilya recommends the selection of officials based on their abilities and qualifications to ensure that the state is governed by competent and worthy administrators rather than officials who might prioritize personal interests over the needs of the state (Kangle, 1965).

Strategies for Combating Corruption

The Arthashastra by Kautilya outlines a range of strategies to prevent and combat corruption, which reflects his belief that the effectiveness of the state depends on the integrity of its officials. Kautilya uses surveillance and intelligence-gathering as one of his primary strategies. He advocated for the appointment of secret agents to monitor the activities of government officials and report observations. The network of secret agents and informants was intended to check on the power of officials and deter them from engaging in corrupt practices out of fear of being caught committing unethical activity (Boesche, 2002).

Kautily's Arthashastra recommended stringent punishments for those guilty of corruption, such as monetary fines, confiscation of property, and even death for officials convicted of embezzlement, bribery, and other corrupt practices. These extreme punishments were designed to deter and discourage officials from committing corrupt activities.

In addition, the Arthashastra highlighted the importance of corruption preventive criteria to fight against corruption. He recommended that officials be regularly rotated in their positions to prevent them from becoming too entrenched and relaxed in their roles, which could offer opportunities for corruption. Rotating officials has proven to be effective in preventing the development of local power bases that could later challenge the authority of the central administration (Rangarajan, 1987).

Aside from the harsh punishment measures, Kautilya advocated for rewards and incentive strategies to promote good behavior among officials. He thought that providing adequate pay and recognizing the achievements of honest and efficient officials would motivate them to continue doing better, which would reduce the temptation to be involved in receiving illegal benefits. His idea of combining positive reinforcement with the threat of punishment was intended to create a balanced system that encouraged integrity and deterred misconduct (Boesche, 2002). This system is still alive in most governments.

Application of Kautilya's Ideas in the Maurya Empire

How much and to what extent the recommendations of Kautilya were applied in the governance of the Maurya Empire is still being studied and debated. The fact that Chandragupta Maurya and his successors seriously took Kautilya's ideas is suggested as evidence of implementation. The principles outlined in the Arthashastra can be observed in the administrative structure of the Maurya Empire, such as the emphasis on centralized control, strict supervision of officials, and the use of intelligence networks.

The administration of the Empire under Chandragupta was overly centralized, with a well-organized bureaucracy that oversaw various aspects of governance, including taxation, law enforcement, and public work projects. The centralization of management allowed the Maurya rules to keep consolidated control over the vast Empire, thus limiting the opportunities for corrupt practices at the provincial level (Thapar, 2002).

Also, the organization of spies and informants to monitor officials was likely employed to ensure that corruption could not undermine the efficiency of the administration, as recommended by Kautilya.

The grandson of Chandragupta, Ashoka, is famous for promoting moral governance and curbing corruption during his rule. As he converted to Buddhism, Ashoka implemented reforms intended to promote ethical behavior among his officials and ensure that they governed the state with principles of justice and compassion. The reforms included the establishment of the Dhamma, a moral code based on Buddhist teachings, and the appointment of 'Dhamma Mahamatras' (officers of morality) to oversee the conduct of officials, are based on the emphasis on integrity in governance by Kautilya (Thapar, 2002).

In sum, the 'Arthashastra' is considered one of the most consequential works on statecraft and governance in ancient civilizations. It detailed strategies for managing corruption within the state, with insights and recommendations that remain relevant in contemporary governance studies. The legacy of the Arthashastra underscores the significance of integrity and accountability in governance, lessons that remain relevant today.

4.4 Persia and the Achaemenid Empire

Founded by Cyrus the Great, the Achaemenid Empire was another classical civilization that suffered the brunt of corruption. The vast Empire and its decentralized administrative system made it susceptible to corrupt practices, particularly among provincial governors ('satraps') and officials within the royal court. The competition for influence and power at the court led to rampant bribery, favoritism, and intrigue, weakening the central authority of the Empire. Let us analyze the impact of corruption on the stability of the Achaemenid Empire, especially in the context of relations, its diverse subjects, and external threats.

Persia and the Achaemenid Empire: Court Intrigues and Corruption

The Achaemenid Empire was founded in the 6th century BCE by Cyrus the Great. The Empire was one of the most powerful empires of the ancient world, encompassing a vast territory stretching from the Balkans and Eastern Europe in the west to the Indus Valley in the east. The Empire had a sophisticated administrative system that made it govern a diverse and expansive domain. However, due to its complexity, various forms of challenges arose, specifically in the form of court intrigues and corruption. Multiple opportunities for corruption among its administrators, governors, and courtiers increased as the Empire expanded. Similar to other chapters, let us explore how corruption within the Achaemenid court and its administrative apparatus undermined the stability of the Empire and contributed to its eventual downfall.

The Role of Satraps in Provincial Governance

The division of the Empire into provinces called 'satrapies' (each governed by a 'satrap') is one of the main characteristics of the Achaemenid administrative system. The 'satraps' were usually the royal family or nobility members who exerted considerable power and authority within their territories. The satraps collected taxes, maintained peace and order, and oversaw local administration. Despite the effectiveness of the satrapal system that allowed the Empire to manage its vast territory, it still created various opportunities for corrupt practices.

The satraps had the autonomy to govern their regions with very little oversight. This autonomy to control over the vast resources made them more prone to corrupt practices, including embezzlement, bribery, and the exploitation of their subjects. Many satraps accumulated immense wealth by diverting state revenues for personal use or charging excessive taxes on the local inhabitants. The corrupt strategies of the satraps not only made them rich and more powerful but also alienated the people they served, leading to discontent and rebellions in some places (Briant, 2002).

Lacking proper oversight by the central government of the Empire exacerbated corruption issues. In trying to curb corruption, the Achaemenid kings, particularly Darius I, implemented unsuccessful measures such as appointing royal inspectors as the "King's Eyes" to monitor the activities of the satraps. Due to the complexity of the administration of the vast Empire, it took much work for the central authority to keep tight control of its provincial governors. Consequently, the persistent problem of corrupt practices by the satraps weakened the cohesion and stability of the Achaemenid Empire (Briant, 2002).

Royal Court Intrigues and Corruption

At the heart of the Achaemenid Empire--the royal court--corruption was rampant as the satraps committed in the provinces. In the royal court, the decisions and judgments of the king could either make or break the careers of nobles, courtiers, and military commanders, among other official positions appointed by the king with decisive authorities and powers. This centralization of power in the court inevitably led to fierce and unfair competition and intrigue as ambitious individuals strived to secure their positions in the government.

During the Achaemenid Empire, the case of Artabanus, a courtier who served as the commander of the royal bodyguard under King Xerxes I, is one of the most familiar examples of court intrigue and corruption.

Artabanus orchestrated the assassination of Xerxes in 465 BCE and attempted to seize power (Briant, 2002). The execution of Artabanus demonstrates the dangers of corruption and intrigues in the royal court as his scheme was foiled and had him executed.

Additionally, the influence of eunuchs in the Achaemenid court fueled the atmosphere of corruption and intrigue. Eunuchs often had significant positions of power within the royal household and were known for political maneuvering and acting as intermediaries between the king and other courtiers. Being close to the king and having control over access to the king were opportunities to manipulate court politics to their benefit, primarily through bribery and the manipulation of information. The corrupt activities of some eunuchs created a culture of favoritism and patronage that produced decisions made based on personal favors rather than merit or the best interest of the state (Sancisi-Weerdenburg, 1989).

Moreover, corruption and intrigues were rampant in royal succession. Corruption issues in the royal succession were significantly due to the lack of a transparent, institutionalized system of succession in the Achaemenid Empire, which usually led to frequent power struggles whenever a king died. Power struggles in claiming the king's seat often involve conspiracies, assassinations, and bribing officials to support the claimant competing over another.

A glaring example is when Darius II died in 404 BCE, Artaxerxes II and

Cyrus the Younger (his two sons) fought defiantly against each other to claim their father's throne. Known as the Battle of Cunaxa in 401, the conflict was fueled by court intrigues and the manipulation of various factions within the Empire. Artaxerxes II ultimately won the battle, underscoring the dangers of corruption and internal division at the highest levels of government, which continued to weaken the Empire (Briant, 2002).

The Impact of Corruption on the Decline of the Achaemenid Empire

The rampant corruption within the Achaemenid administration and royal court had debilitating impacts on the stability and prosperity of the Empire. Overall, corruption eroded the effectiveness of governance as decisions were increasingly made based on personal benefits only.

Corruption in the provinces caused the alienation of the subjects of the Empire. It weakened the cohesion between the central government and its territories, which made it more challenging for the Achaemenid kings to sustain control.

Corruption caused a financial strain on the administration, disabling the Empire from standing strong and sustainable. The embezzlement of state revenues and other corrupt practices reduced the resources crucial to sustaining the central government, making it harder to fund the military, public works, and other essential features of the Empire to function properly. The external aggressions, such as the invasions by Alexander the Great in the late 4th century BCE, worsened the financial weakness of the Achaemenid Empire (Briant, 2002).

Alexander the Great successfully subdued the Achaemenid Empire, taking advantage of the Empire's internal divisions and weaknesses caused by corruption. To achieve his victory, Alexander exploited the discontent among the subjects and the rivalries within the ruling class of the Empire. The Achaemenid Empire's collapse in 330 BCE was caused not only by external forces but also by the corrosive impacts of corruption within its ranks that facilitated the victory of the Macedonian king, Alexander.

In other words, the fight of the Achaemenid Empire against corruption and court intrigues highlighted the challenges of developing and establishing excellent governance strategies. Despite efforts to manage their territories, pervasive corruption weakened the Empire's institutions, alienated its subjects, and hindered its ability to address external threats. The decline of the Empire serves as a cautionary story about the menaces of corruption and the importance of integrity in governance.

References

Boesche, R. (2002). *The First Great Political Realist: Kautilya and His Arthashastra.* Lexington Books.

Briant, P. (2002). *From Cyrus to Alexander: A History of the Persian Empire.* Eisenbrauns.

Finley, M. I. (1973). *Democracy Ancient and Modern.* Rutgers University Press.

Gruen, E. S. (1974). *The Last Generation of the Roman Republic.* University of California Press.

Kangle, R. P. (1965). *The Kautilya Arthashastra, Part 2: An English Translation with Critical and Explanatory Notes.* University of Bombay.

Ober, J. (1989). *Mass and Elite in Democratic Athens: Rhetoric, Ideology, and the Power of the People.* Princeton University Press.

Ostrogorsky, G. (1969). *History of the Byzantine State.* Rutgers University Press.

Rangarajan, L. N. (1987). *Kautilya: The Arthashastra.* Penguin Classics.

Sancisi-Weerdenburg, H. (1989). *Achaemenid Empire's History III: Method and Theory.* Leiden University Press.

Syme, R. (1939). *The Roman Revolution.* Oxford University Press.

Tacitus. (1999). *The Annals of Imperial Rome (M. Grant, Trans.).* Penguin Classics.

Thapar, R. (2002). *Asoka and the Decline of the Mauryas* (3rd ed.). Oxford University Press.

Treadgold, W. (1997). *A History of the Byzantine State and Society.* Stanford University Press.

CHAPTER 5.

MEDIEVAL CORRUPTION

5.1. Feudal Europe: Nobility, Bribery, and the Church's Role

The medieval period in Europe (5th - 15th century) was dominated by a socio-political system known as feudalism. The lords owned vast tracts of land, which provided them with wealth and power that controlled their vassals and peasants. This was a master-servant relationship that characterized the hierarchical feudal system. The decentralized nature of feudalism proved its weakness as it inherently facilitated corruption, especially among the nobility and within the Church, which are factors that wield immense influence over the populace.

Feudal Lords and Corruption

The lords dominated the feudal medieval hierarchy by controlling vast tracts of land granted by monarchs in exchange for military service. The peasants, or serfs, who tilled the lands were legally bound to the lords of the estates. The lords exploited their vassals and serfs, using the power dynamics in this relationship to skew in their favor. The unfair practices included the imposition of illegal taxes, the seizure of common lands, and the arbitrary administration of justice.

In addition, manipulating feudal obligations was one consequential form of corruption. The lords often abused the system instead of protecting and giving provisions for their vassals who served them as military. Lords exploited the vassals, demanding excessive and burdensome services or payments more than customary. Feudal lords abused their power, extending to the administration of justice by acting as judges within their domain. Due to the lack of a centralized legal system, these lords could wield judicial power arbitrarily by using their courts to settle personal disputes or extort wealth from those under their jurisdiction (Bloch, 1961).

Furthermore, the loyalty and military service that the feudal system emphasized often led to corruption, especially when allocating titles and land. It was a typical corrupt practice to grant noble titles and estates in exchange for bribes or other forms of benefit rather than on the merit of the service of the recipient. This practice more often led to internal conflict, sabotaging the integrity of the feudal hierarchy as it treated loyalty as a commodity rather than a merit (Bloch, 1961).

Church Corruption

The medieval Church, one of the most powerful institutions in Europe during this period, was not immune to corruption. The Church possessed significant temporal power, possessing vast tracks of land and wealth.

Nevertheless, the vast resources and influence often led to moral decay and the widespread practice of 'Simony,' a practice of doing business outside ecclesiastical offices (Duffy, 1997). Simony was rampant during the 10th and 11th centuries, particularly when the wealthy aspired to secure high-ranking positions within the Church, such as bishoprics and abbeys. Their aim was not for spiritual reasons but to gain control over church lands and revenues.

The sale of indulgences was another major corrupt practice within the Church. The original intention of indulgences was for the faithful to reduce their time in purgatory through acts of penance. However, indulgences became a commodity, with the Church selling indulgences to raise funds during the Crusades by the later Middle Ages. Exploiting spiritual beliefs through indulgences has enriched the Church, which became severe and led to disillusionment among the laity, which was resonated with by the Protestant

Reformation movement (Herrin, 2008).

Just as it exists in the political sphere, Nepotism was another form of corruption prevalent within the Church. This corrupt practice was prevalent in granting Church offices to relatives of powerful clergy regardless of their qualifications or religious vocation, which eventually deteriorated the moral authority of the Church (Duffy, 1997).

The monastic orders were not spared from being corrupted despite their practice of spiritual ideals of poverty and piety. Many monasteries became morally and financially corrupt as they accumulated massive wealth and resources. Notably, some abbots and monks became more focused on managing their estates and accruing their wealth than their spiritual duties. This shift from spiritual to temporal often led to the exploitation of the laity through taxing or coercing them into working on monastic lands (Bloch, 1961).

Corruption in the medieval period within the nobility and the Church had far-reaching impacts, including deterioration of social order and internal conflicts. The abuses of power and moral decays brought about through the feudal system underscored its intrinsic weaknesses. However, the series of events in that period set the stage for the transformative evolutions of the late Middle Ages and the Renaissance.

5.2. The Byzantine Empire: Bureaucratic Corruption and Its Consequences

Lasting from the fall of the Western Roman Empire (476 CE) until the conquest of Constantinople (1453), the Byzantine Empire was known for its complex and sophisticated administrative system. The Empire's bureaucracy was vital to its prosperity and governance. However, history tells us that its bureaucracy was also the breeding ground for corruption. The complicated administration and the tremendous authority vested in the officials often led them to abuse their powers. The abuse of power and authority negatively impacted the effectiveness of the system, which led to the eventual collapse of the Empire.

Administrative Corruption

The bureaucracy of the Byzantine Empire was considered one of the most elaborate in the medieval world, a system that featured a highly centralized form of governance with power concentrated in the hands of the emperor and his officials. The emperor-appointed officials managed everything from tax collection to the administration of justice, often giving them opportunities for aggrandizement. This bureaucratic system opened opportunities for corruption manifested in various forms, including embezzlement, bribery, and manipulating laws and justice for personal benefit.

The embezzlement of state funds by officials was gained through siphoning off a portion of the revenues before sending the remainder of the tax collected to the imperial treasury. Embezzlement not only deprived the need of the state of many resources but also added a heavier burden on the citizens who were taxed beyond their capacity to compensate for the losses. Writing in the 11th century, historian Michael Psellus often criticized the crooked and greedy bureaucrats who, despite their loyalty to the emperor, enriched themselves at the expense of the state (Herrin, 2008).

Official administrators often resort to bribery to advance their careers or secure lucrative positions because they possess many favors and influence within the imperial court. From minor clerks to high-ranking officials, the culture of bribery extended to all levels of the system and created an environment where merit and competence were irrelevant and often secondary to wealth and connections. Bribery was a pervasive integrity issue that eroded the efficiency of the administration, making the public cynical and dubious of the government's credibility (Kazhdan & Epstein, 1985).

Taxation and Corruption

Funding the military campaigns, public works, and the lavish lifestyle of the imperial court require massive taxes as the lifeblood of the Byzantine Empire. However, the tax collection system is riddled with corruption by 'praktor' (tax collectors), notorious for inflating assessments and pocketing the difference, causing the populace to be overburdened and impoverished. This corrupt tax collection practice was particularly harmful during the wars between the Empire and its neighbors and other times of crisis when the revenue was most needed.

The long-term consequence of corruption within the tax system impacted the social and economic stability of the Empire as peasants were forced to abandon their lands, causing a decline in agricultural productivity and a decrease in state revenues because of the burden of increasing taxes. The decline of tax collection was also aggravated by the 'dynatoi', the powerful class of landowners who evaded taxes by using their wealth and influence or by shifting the burden onto the poorer citizens (Kazhdan, 1999). Just like in other great empires, the resulting reality of the economic inequalities in the state contributed to social unrest and led to the incapacity of the Empire to win or at least resist external threats.

The Role of the Eparch

The Eparch of Constantinople was responsible for the administration of the capital city. Some vital duties were overseeing the markets, regulating the city's guilds, maintaining public order, and ensuring grain supply to the population. The highly coveted position of the Eparch means that it was highly susceptible to unfair competition or, worse, corruption, given that Constantinople was the political and economic heart of the Empire.

The Eparchs were particularly detrimental to the lives of the citizens in the capital city as they practiced corruption, manipulating market prices, granting monopolies to favored merchants, and extorting bribes from guilds and traders. These and other corrupt activities have made the Eparch and his associates wealthy but have also negatively disrupted the economy and fueled discontent among the citizens. Writing in the 11th century, the chronicler Jonh Skylitzes described that "justice was sold to the highest bidder," illustrating the deep-seated corruption pervasive in the office of the Eparch in Constantinople (Kazhdan, 1999).

Military Corruption

The military of the Byzantine Empire was not immune to corruption. Due to corruption, maintaining a large and effective army became increasingly difficult as the Empire expanded and contracted over the centuries.

Embezzling the pay of the soldiers, selling military positions not based on merit, and providing substandard equipment and supplies were instances of several forms of corruption within the military.

Embezzling funds allotted for the army had directly sabotaged the military capabilities of the Empire. Soldiers often felt demoralized and became less effective in battle as they were not paid on time or received less than they deserved. The corrupt practice of selling military positions meant that high military positions were often filled by individuals with wealth rather than competence, experience, and expertise, weakening the military capability of the Empire. Combined with the lack of proper military supplies, this situation resulted in the decline of military leadership and many disastrous battle defeats (Ostrogorsky, 1969).

Also, designed to decentralize military and civil administration to protect the borders of the Empire, the Byzantine Theme system became a source of corruption. The 'strategoi' (local commanders) were granted greater autonomy over their regions, including the authority to collect taxes and sustain local militias. The situation opened the local commanders to opportunities to abuse their autonomy and power to enrich themselves at the expense of the state. Due to the corrupt practices within the Theme system, the defenses of the Empire weakened and contributed to the loss of main territories, especially in defending against threats from the Arabs, Bulgars, and Seljuk Turks (Treadgold, 1997).

Consequences of Corruption

The impacts of corruption in the Byzantine Empire were fatal and far-reaching. The corrupt officials who bred inefficiencies and injustice eroded the legitimacy of the imperial government and caused social unrest. The corruption in taxation and military administration caused an economic disruption, weakening the ability of the state to respond to internal and external challenges. Over time, these issues pushed the Empire to its eventual deterioration, making it more susceptible to external aggression and internal strife.

Moreover, structural corruption within the Byzantine bureaucracy brought the Empire to the centralization of authority and control among the few influential elites, which led to the marginalization of the broader and larger population. The concentration of power within the few elites resulted in short-term stability but at the cost of long-term resilience and prosperity. The dependence of the Empire on a corrupt and self-serving elite ultimately damaged its capability to adapt to changing circumstances, thus being handicapped to confront the challenges of the later Medieval period.

Conclusion

The sophisticated bureaucracy of the Byzantine Empire shows its strength during that period. However, as the system allowed for the administration of a vast and diverse empire, the strength itself became its own weakness, leading the way to opportunistic elites to take advantage of and gain personal wealth. The pervasive nature and culture of corruption negatively impacted the economic, military, and social stability of the Empire, which caused its eventual decline and downfall.

5.3. Islamic Caliphates: Corruption in Governance and Justice

From the 7th to the 13th centuries, the Islamic Caliphates presented a golden age of Islamic civilization, featuring incredible achievements in science, culture, governance, and more fields. Like many other vast empires in the medieval world, the Caliphates were not immune to the challenges of corruption. Islam has foundational teachings emphasizing justice, honesty, and accountability; however, corruption permeated various levels of governance and the judicial system, which were prominent during the Umayyad and Abbasid periods. This corruption sabotaged the moral and political authority of the Islamic rulers and caused internal strife and the downfall of the caliphates.

Corruption in the Umayyad Caliphate

Marking the first prominent Islamic dynasty, the Umayyad Caliphate (661-750 CE) succeeded the Rashidun Caliphate. During the Umayyad Caliphate, the Islamic Empire rapidly expanded, bringing immense wealth and power to the ruling class. However, it also brought considerable challenges in sustaining effective governance over diverse and far-flung territories of the Empire. The Umayyad caliphs and their network of governors ('walis') centralized the power to administer the provinces, which created opportunities for corruption among themselves.

The accumulation of wealth and power by provincial governors, mostly family members of the caliphs or close associates, was one of the major forms of corruption during the Umayyad period. These provincial governors abused their broad authority to amass personal fortunes, mainly gained from taxation, justice, and military affairs. Their wealth was gained through practices such as collecting excessive taxes from non-Muslim populations ('dhimmis'), embezzling public funds, and manipulating legal rulings to favor their interests (Lapidus, 2014).

The Umayyad caliphs and their governors lived lavish lifestyles in contrast to the egalitarian principles of the early Island, which led to widespread discontent among the subjects of the Empire. This discontent grew worse among the non-Arab Muslim converts ('mawali'), who were often treated as second-class citizens despite their religious status. Due to this perceived corruption and favoritism within the Umayyad administration, the opposition against the dynasty aggravated, culminating in the Abbasid Revolution of 750 CE (Kennedy, 2004).

The Abbasid Caliphate and Bureaucratic Corruption

When Baghdad became a center of learning and culture, the Abbasid Caliphate (750-1258 CE) was often regarded as the pinnacle of Islamic civilization, especially during its early centuries. However, due to the vastness of the Empire and the complexity of its bureaucracy, an environment of corruption developed. The caliphate relied on an overarching administrative apparatus to control its diverse territories, often delegated to regional governors, viziers (high-ranking advisors), and other officials.

These governors and officials were notorious for manipulating the tax system during the Abbasid period. Taxation was the lifeblood of revenue for the caliphate, funding the military campaigns and public works of the Empire. The taxation system was highly susceptible to corrupt practices by tax collectors and governors who were performing their official roles far from the central authority in Baghdad. These officials continually over-taxed the local populations and pocketed the excess, which led to widespread economic hardship and resentment among the subjects of the Empire (Lapidus, 2014).

The position of the chief administrative officer (vizier), who often wields enormous authority, also became a role tempting corrupt individuals to grab the opportunity. The infamous vizier Al-Fadl iban Sahl, during the reign of Caliph Al-Ma'mun, accumulated vast wealth by exploiting their official role.

They appointed relatives and allies to critical positions and accepted bribes in exchange for political favors and other forms of Nepotism and corruption in general terms. The accumulation of wealth and concentration of power by the elites contributed to factionalism within the court as rival factions competed for authority over the resources of the caliphate (Kennedy, 2004).

The Decline of the Abbasid Caliphate

In the later years of the Abbasid Caliphate, corruption was becoming entrenched, exacerbating the decline of the Empire. Being isolated but reliant on their military commanders (known as Mamluks, often Turkic slaves), the caliphs struggled to maintain control over their Empire. As the commanders embezzled funds allocated to the army, corruption within the military became more problematic, leading to underpaid soldiers and a poorly equipped army. Again, this corrupt practice weakened the ability of the Islamic Empire to prevent external threats, particularly from the Seljuk Turks and the Crusaders (Lapidus, 2014).

In addition, corruption has significant economic consequences. The mismanagement of the tax system and embezzlement of public funds led to financial crises. The decline of revenue undermined the stability of the Empire. It forced the caliphs to debase the currency and increase taxes, which worsened the burden and the discontent of the population. The economic crises were the main factor that caused the fragmentation of the caliphate, as the regional governors and military commanders claimed their independence and established their rival states (Kennedy, 2004).

Islamic Legal Thought on Corruption

Islamic law, or Sharia, is fundamentally grounded in principles of justice, honesty, and the equal treatment of individuals. The Q'uran explicitly condemns bribery (referred to as 'rishwa') and other corrupt practices, aside from emphasizing the importance of accountability in governance. Nevertheless, the enforcement of Sharia varies across different periods and regions of the caliphatic world.

Significant efforts were made to combat corruption within the judicial system where the Islamic judges (called 'qadis') were the justice administrators according to Sharia during the Abbasid period. Nevertheless, corruption was pervasive within the judiciary. Some qadis accepted bribes from wealthy or influential individuals in exchange for favorable rulings. These corrupt practices undermined the integrity of the judicial system and eroded public trust in the capability of the caliphate to uphold justice (Kennedy, 2004).

Despite the challenges, there were also attempts to resolve corruption within the Islamic legal framework. Such attempts by the Abbasid Caliph Al-Mansur, for example, attempted to reform and curb corruption among provincial governors and tax collectors, including the creation of a checks and balances system. Despite the efforts, the reforms, particularly in the distant provinces of the Empire, proved to be more challenging to enforce (Lapidus, 2014)

Corruption in governance and injustice led to the decline of the Islamic Caliphates, creating economic, social, and political instability. This weakened the caliphates and made them vulnerable to internal fragmentation and external threats. The legacy of this corruption serves as a reminder of the challenges of maintaining effective governance in large and diverse states.

5.4. Feudal Japan: Samurai, Daimyo, and Corruption in the Shogunate

Spanning from the 12th century until the Meiji Restoration in 1868, Feudal Japan was under a rigid hierarchical structure where power was decentralized among military leaders known as 'daimyo' and their vassals, the 'samurai.' The Tokugawa Shogunate (1603--1868) was remarkably politically and socially stable during this period. Despite the overall stable atmosphere of the

Shogunate, it was also when corruption became deeply entrenched within the structures of power, especially among the samurai and daimyo, and within the administration of the Shogunate. The issues of corruption undermined the integrity of the Japanese feudal system, contributing to the fall of the Tokugawa regime.

Samurai Corruption

Initially serving as warriors of daimyo, the samurai gradually evolved into bureaucratic roles as the Tokugawa period ushered longer peace. Although the samurai class was traditionally bound by the code of 'bushido' (emphasizing a code of honor, loyalty, and martial virtue), the present realities of their roles often make them leave those ideals. Most samurais faced economic pressures as they were usually paid rice stipends that did not keep pace with inflation. This oppressing situation often drives them to engage in corrupt activities to keep their status and livelihoods (Totman, 1980).

The samurai engaged in corruption by exploiting the peasants as administrative officials responsible for collecting taxes and managing local affairs. Due to the lack of adequate oversight, the samurais took the opportunity to demand excessive taxes or extort bribes from the peasantry in exchange for favors. These forms of exploitation not only impoverished the peasants but also eroded the moral authority of the samurai class as they became to be seen as oppressors rather than protectors (Turnbull, 2012)

The duties of the samurai also led to the erosion of bushido as it became commercialized. Many samurais began lending money at high interest rates or engaging in trade, which was forbidden under the strict social codes of the time. Engaging in various pursuits of profit over duty was a clear departure from the ideals of bushido, which contributed to the moral decline of the samurai class (Totman, 1980).

Daimyo and Shogunate Corruption

The daimyo were powerful feudal lords ruling with greater autonomy under the authority of the shogun, and they controlled vast territories in Japan. The Tokugawa Shogunate implemented an administrative system called 'sankin-kotai', or alternate attendance. The system required the daimyo to spend every other year in Edo (Tokyo) to prevent the daimyo from amassing significant power in their own domains and ensuring their loyalty to the Shogunate. On the contrary, this system opened opportunities for corruption both within the governance of the daimyo and with the administration of the Shogunate (Jansen, 2000).

Manipulating the 'sankin-kotai' system was one of the forms of corruption among the daimyo. Managing a residence in Edo, traveling back and forth, and maintaining their domains was costly for the daimyo, which led them to impose additional taxes on their subjects or engage in other corrupt activities. The corrupt practices had burdened the local population, which led to resentment towards both the daimyo and the Shogunate (Totman, 1980).

Additionally, daimyo are often involved in Nepotism and favoritism with their relatives and close associates. Due to nepotism and favoritism practices, the effectiveness of governance was undermined, leading to widespread inefficiencies and abuses of power. Since there was a lack of a central authority to oversee the appointment methods, the daimyo could freely rule their domains with greater autonomy, often at the disadvantage of their subjects (Jansen, 2000).

The Tokugawa Shogunate was not immune to corruption, and their efforts to maintain strict control over the daimyo and samurai failed due to the corrupt practices even within the administration of the Shogunate.

For example, the 'roju' (senior counselors) and 'bugyo' (magistrates) high-ranking officers were often implicated in bribery, the sale of offices, and the manipulation of judicial decisions. These officials used their positions and power to amass personal wealth at the expense of justice and good governance (Totman, 1980).

Anti-Corruption Reforms and Their Limitations

Shoguns implemented reforms to curb corruption and restore the integrity of the administration during the Edo period. For instance, the 'Kyoho Reforms' implemented by Shogun Tokugawa Yoshimune in the early 18th century attempted to address economic mismanagement and bureaucratic corruption. The reforms had measures that audited the finances of the Shogunate, reduced unnecessary expenditures, and provided more stringent oversight of officials (Totman, 1980).

Although the reforms achieved some successes in stabilizing the economy and reducing the pervasiveness of corruption, they were ultimately limited in scope. The pervasive corrupt activities within the samurais and daimyo classes, aggravated by the rigid social hierarchy that protected the ruling elite, made it very challenging to enact more comprehensive changes. In addition, focusing on keeping social order and preventing dissent often took precedence over efforts to curb corruption, perpetuating the status quo (Jansen, 2000).

The Decline of the Tokugawa Shogunate

The pervasive corruption issues within the samurai, daimyo, and Shogunate eventually led to the downfall of the Tokugawa regime.

In addition to the costs associated with maintaining control over the daimyo and the increasing demands of the samurai class, the Shogunate became more reliant on excessive taxes and loans as the financial pressures grew. This economic strain exacerbated social instability, leading to samurai discontent and peasant revolts.

Moreover, the failure of the Shogunate to effectively address corruption and enforce meaningful reforms eroded its authority and legitimacy.

The inability of Japan to govern and defend the country exposed the Tokugawa regime to its weaknesses when the Western powers arrived and forced open its ports by the mid-19th century. The internal and external challenges ultimately brought down the Shogunate, which led to the restoration of imperial rule under Emperor Meiji in 1868 (Jansen, 2000).

Corruption within feudal Japan, particularly among the samurai, daimyo, and Shogunate, sabotaged the stability of the Tokugawa regime. Efforts to reform were hindered by deeply embedded corrupt practices and a rigid social hierarchy, contributing to the tensions that led to the Meiji Restoration and modernization of Japan.

References

Bloch, M. (1961). *Feudal Society, Volume 1: The Growth of Ties of Dependence*. University of Chicago Press.

Duffy, E. (1997). *Saints and Sinners: A History of the Popes*. Yale University Press.

Herrin, J. (2008). *Byzantium: The Surprising Life of a Medieval Empire*. Princeton University Press.

Jansen, M. B. (2000). *The Making of Modern Japan*. Harvard University Press.

Kazhdan, A. P., & Epstein, A. W. (1985). *Change in Byzantine Culture in the Eleventh and Twelfth Centuries*. University of California Press.

Kazhdan, A. P. (1999). *The Oxford Dictionary of Byzantium*. Oxford University Press.

Kennedy, H. (2004). *The Prophet and the Age of the Caliphates: The Islamic Near East from the Sixth to the Eleventh Century*. Longman.

Lapidus, I. M. (2014). *A History of Islamic Societies (3rd ed.)*. Cambridge University Press.

Ostrogorsky, G. (1969). *History of the Byzantine State*. Rutgers University Press.

Totman, C. D. (1980). *The Collapse of the Tokugawa Bakufu, 1862-1868*. University of Hawaii Press.

Treadgold, W. (1997). *A History of the Byzantine State and Society*. Stanford University Press.

Turnbull, S. (2012). *Samurai: The World of the Warrior*. Osprey Publishing.

CHAPTER 6.

THE ROLE OF CORRUPTION IN THE DECLINE OF CIVILIZATIONS

6.1. How Corruption Undermines Governance

Throughout history, corruption has been a persistent issue undermining good governance and contributing to the collapse of great ancient civilizations. Corruption corrodes power structures, weakens institutions, and erodes public trust in government. Corruption negatively impacts governance, affecting everything from the administration of justice to the economic management of the delivery of public goods and services. We will examine how corruption sabotages governance by exploring its effects on political stability, economic performance, social cohesion, and the legitimacy of authorities.

Erosion of Political Stability

Erosion of political integrity is one of the most detrimental impacts of corruption on governance. The effectiveness of governance depends on the legitimacy of the authorities and the trust the citizens place in them. As corruption becomes systemic, it sabotages trust, making citizens disillusioned and cynical, leading to social unrest. When citizens perceive corruption in leadership, they tend to refrain from complying with laws, paying taxes, or engaging in civic activities. Such non-compliance would deteriorate the social understanding between the state and its citizens (Rose-Ackerman, 1999).

Corruption also breeds political instability by nurturing a climate of uncertainty and unpredictability. Corrupt leaders often prioritize their personal ambitions over the public good, make arbitrary decisions, and manipulate legal and political processes. Such leaders are inconsistent in policy-making and enforcement and wield power either as alone individuals or as a faction. The resulting instability not only damages the effectiveness of governance but also opens opportunities for rival groups to challenge the authority, leading to factionalism, coups, or even civil war (Acemoglu & Robinson, 2012).

Numerous historical corruption cases are testaments that directly contributed to the political instability and the decline of past great civilizations. For instance, the Roman Empire had widespread corruption among their officials that eroded civic virtue, playing a significant role in the instability of the Empire to maintain effective governance. The state has weakened in responding to external threats and internal challenges due to constant infighting, bribery, and manipulation within the Roman Senate and imperial court that eventually brought the Empire to its downfall (Syme, 1939).

Economic Mismanagement and Inefficiency

Corruption can sabotage good governance by leading to economic mismanagement and inefficiency. Whenever public officials engage in the embezzling of funds, accepting bribes, awarding contracts based on favoritism rather than merit, and other corrupt practices, the allotment of resources becomes distorted. Rather than employing to promoting the public good, finance and other resources were diverted to serving the personal interests of a corrupt elite, leading to inefficiencies, waste, and reduction of economic development (Mauro, 1995)

The impact on public procurement is one of the substantial ways in which corruption affects economic governance. In many cases, government contracts are awarded to those who offer the largest bribes or have the closest connections to officials but not to the most qualified or cost-effective bidders. Such corrupt behavior leads to substandard infrastructure construction, delivering low-quality public services and utilities, and misallocating public funds. In the long run, this corrupt practice would undermine the ability of the state to provide for its citizens, which can erode public confidence in the capacity of the government to manage the economy efficiently and effectively (Shleifer & Vishny, 1993).

Corruption also sabotages tax collection, which is a critical component of economic governance. Corrupt government officials, such as tax officers, accept bribes from companies or individuals in exchange for underreporting taxable income, granting tax exemptions, or allowing friends to evade tax burdens. These corrupt tax officials decrease the state revenues, thus hindering the state's capability to sustain education, healthcare, and infrastructure development among the fundamental social services and public facilities. The shortage in public investment can lead to economic stagnation, recession, increased poverty, and a widening gap between the rich and the poor (Friedman et al., 2000).

Weakening of Institutions and the Rule of Law

Pervasive corruption in society undermines governance by weakening institutions and eroding the rule of law. Without corruption, institutions are potent and compelling and serve as the backbone of any well-governed society, providing the frameworks within which economic, political, and social activities occur. However, when corruption is normalized in these institutions, their ability to function effectively is compromised, which could break the rule of law and deteriorate social order (North, 1990).

In various circumstances, judicial corruption occurs, where judges and law enforcement officials take bribes to influence legal outcomes. This form of corruption undermines the impartiality of the justice system, which could lead to creating an environment where criminals and offenders can buy justice. Citizens will resort to alternative means of resolving disputes, such as violence or vigilantism, when they lose faith in the capability of the judiciary to uphold the law, which will destabilize society (Rose-Ackerman, 1999).

Most of all, when corruption erodes law enforcement agencies and they begin to enforce laws selectively, specific individuals or groups can act with impunity while others are wrongly penalized. This situation will not only perpetuate inequality and injustice but also create an atmosphere of lawlessness, where the rule of power and influence replaces the rule of law. In such a situation, proper governance will be very challenging as the state loses its monopoly on its legitimate use of force and ability to maintain and preserve order (Acemoglu & Robinson, 2012).

Erosion of Legitimacy and Public Trust

Most probably, the most profound way corruption undermines governance is by eroding the legitimacy of the ruling authorities and the trust the citizens place in them. Legitimacy is the foundation of the authority of a government and the only element that authorizes the state and gives it the right to govern and the people the willingness to be governed.

Widespread corruption in the government signals to the public that particular government officials or institutions are more concerned with benefiting the interests of a corrupt aristocracy than with advancing the common good of society. This behavior can lead to a crisis of legitimacy, where the citizens no longer perceive the government as a legitimate and effective representative of their interests (Levi, 1997).

When the public trust in the government erodes, its citizens may become less likely to obey national laws, pay taxes, or participate in civic activities. This environment of distrust can create a vicious cycle where the integrity of the state is weakened, leading to more corruption, worsening public disillusionment, and increasing overall instability. In extreme historical cases, the loss of legitimacy can lead to the collapse of the state as its citizens withdraw support or actively resist the government, which could pave the way for revolution, civil war, or even foreign intervention (Acemoglu & Robinson, 2012).

In sum, corruption undermines governance by corroding political stability and economic efficiency, which could weaken legal institutions and establishments that serve the common good of the citizens. Corruption in the government is a moral and ethical deterioration that betrays public trust in leaders and institutions. Addressing corruption is paramount for revitalizing trust and legitimacy in governance.

6.2. Economic Corruption and Resource Misallocation

Economic corruption is typically described as the misuse of public office for private gain. It is a type of corruption that played a destructive role in the downfall of civilizations by distorting economic processes, leading to the misallocation of funds and other public resources. Additionally, when economic corruption infiltrates the economic systems of a state, it sabotages efficiency, hampers growth, and aggravates inequality in a stable and prosperous society.

In this chapter, we will explore how economic corruption and resource misallocation have factually and historically brought down great civilizations, drawing on both historical examples and contemporary analyses to illustrate the impact of corruption on economic systems.

The Mechanisms of Economic Corruption

The mechanisms of economic corruption occur in the form of bribery, embezzlement, nepotism, favoritism, and fraud. These practices distort the allocation of funds and other public resources by diverting them from their intended uses to benefit the interests of corrupt officials and their surrogates and associates. Where corruption is widespread, decisions about resource allocation, including the awarding of contracts, the distribution of public funds, or the granting of licenses, are often concluded based on personal connections, bribes, or political favoritism rather than merit or efficiency (Shleifer & Vishny, 1993).

There are various adverse economic impacts of misallocations of resources. First, it leads to the decline of the overall efficiency of the economy by allocating resources to less productive and substandard projects. When a government contract is awarded to a firm based on bribery rather than capability, the quality of public infrastructure, services, and goods will likely suffer. The awarded contractor will haphazardly build roads, bridges, and buildings, misusing public funds and hindering economic activities with substandard structures, which would incur increasing costs for repairs and reduce productivity. These inefficient impacts ultimately stifle economic growth and development (Mauro, 1995).

Second, companies will compete with each other to expend additional resources on bribes and other illicit payments to secure contracts or avoid regulatory barriers as the economic corruption situation increases. This economic corruption scenario creates a less competitive business environment as firms that are reluctant or unable to engage in corrupt practices may be excluded from markets or opportunities. The lack of an equal playing field (EPF) of business competition can lead to higher prices, lower quality goods and services, and reduced innovation, negatively impacting economic growth (Rose-Ackerman & Palifka, 2016).

Historical Resource Misallocation Due to Corruption Examples

Economic corruption played a crucial part in the downfall of civilizations through the misappropriation of resources. The Roman Empire, for example, has shown that corruption can undermine economic stability and could eventually destroy any great civilization. Corruption was rampant within the Roman Empire during its later years, particularly in the administration of public funds and the allocation of resources. Many Roman tax collectors and provincial governors, among other corrupt officials, often embezzled funds and took bribes, which logically diverted resources away from essential public service and infrastructure projects (Syme, 1939).

This economic corruption severely impacted the Roman Empire. As the officials siphoned off public funds, it negatively impacted the Empire's ability to maintain its vast network of roads, aqueducts, and vital infrastructures. Some of the impacts of corruption led to the deterioration of infrastructure quality and number hindered trade, communication, and military mobility, affecting the economic and defensive capabilities of the Empire. In addition, the social unrest and destabilization of the Empire were exacerbated as citizens were negatively affected by the heavy tax burdens imposed on them to compensate for the lost revenue due to corruption (Jones, 1964).

Another monumental example is the economic corruption the great Qing Dynasty in China faced during its later years. In particular, the corruption in the administration of taxes and public works of the imperial bureaucracy opened to pervasive resource misappropriation. Many local officials collected excessive taxes from peasants, underreported the amounts to the central government, and pocketed the difference. These malpractices in tax collection had severely impoverished the rural population, depriving them of rendering taxes due to the state and consequentially depriving resources to fund military defenses, public works, and other vital governance functions. Ultimately, such economic strain contributed to the weakening and eventual decline of the Qing Dynasty in the early 20th century (Huang, 1996).

Contemporary Implications of Economic Corruption

Economic corruption persists as a considerable barrier to development and a contributor to the decline of states in the modern period. Nations and territories with high levels of corruption indeed suffer slower economic growth, higher levels of poverty, and dreadful inequality at various levels. This situation is created by corruption that significantly distorts market mechanisms, creating inefficient public spending and damaging the trust of both domestic and international investors (World Bank, 2020).

For example, corruption in the public sector in many developing countries leads to the misappropriation of resources intended for vital areas such as education, healthcare, and infrastructure. In such an environment, funds earmarked for schools, hospitals, and roads are mostly diverted to private or personal accounts or spent on unplanned (unapproved) projects benefiting only officials rather than the public. This misappropriation of resources has long-term negative impacts on human capital development, economic productivity, and social prosperity, which results in a vicious cycle of poverty and underdevelopment (Rose-Ackerman & Palifka, 2016).

Some resource-rich countries have fallen victim to the "resource curse," where abundant natural resources lead to economic corruption manifesting in various forms. Such countries included those that generate national wealth from natural resources, including oil or minerals, primarily managed and controlled by a few elites. At the same time, the broader population remains impoverished and has no opportunities to benefit from natural wealth. Ross (2012) described that the misallocation of resource wealth would exacerbate inequality and stifle economic diversification, making these resource curse countries more vulnerable to economic shocks and contributing to long-term economic decline.

Preventing Corruption and Resource Misallocation

Only institutions with strong integrity characters can ensure that resources are allocated efficiently and equitably and prevent economic corruption in the long run. Such institutions should possess independent judiciaries, transparent procurement systems, and robust regulatory frameworks, which can prevent opportunities for corruption and increase accountability and oversight. Strong institutions usually have implemented rigorous anti-corruption measures, including competitive bidding processes for government contracts and the disclosure of the assets of public officials, and have existing and visible improvements in the allocation of resources and overall economic performance (North, 1990).

Additionally, it is crucial for civil society and the media to diligently and bravely expose corruption and hold officials accountable for their actions. Public disclosures of corrupt practices by public officials and private heads have led to reforms that promote good governance and reduce resource misappropriation among governments, businesses, and institutions. According to the World Bank, advocacy by non-governmental organizations (NGOs) and investigative journalists has been instrumental in exposing corruption scandals and pushing for greater transparency and accountability in the public and private sectors (World Bank, 2020).

In short, economic corruption and resource misallocation (or misappropriation) have historically brought great civilizations to their eventual downfall and provided us with glaring insights on how to govern our present societies to prosper in every respect. Corruption distorts resource allocation, weakens economic efficiency, inhibits growth, and exacerbates inequality in various forms. Robust institutions, effective oversight, and civil society involvement are a must to address corruption and ensure resources are allotted for the public good.

6.3. Social Corruption and the Erosion of Trust

Broadly defined as the degradation of ethical norms and social values due to corrupt practices, social corruption plays a considerable role in the decline of civilizations. As corruption infiltrates a society, it sabotages good governance and economic efficiency and corrodes the social fabric by destroying the trust that binds communities together. Trust is the foundation of social cohesion that, when broken, would result in widespread cynicism, breakdown in social cooperation, and ultimately, fragmentation of society. Let us examine how social corruption factors erode trust and how this process historically precipitated the downfall of the great civilizations we know.

The Role of Trust in Social Cohesion

Trust factor is the bedrock of any well-functioning society. The central function of trust is that it supports cooperation, facilitates economic transactions, and underpins the legitimacy of social institutions. Social trust means the confidence that individuals have in each other, in their leaders, and in the institutions that govern their present and future lives. There is evidence of high levels of trust if there are numerous positive outcomes, such as greater civic engagement, more effective governance, and higher levels of economic expansion (Putnam, 2000).

People are more likely to work together to achieve common visions, resolve conflicts amicably, and comply with social norms and laws when there is strong trust. Contrarily, social cooperation breaks down, and people become more inclined to be selfish at the expense of the collective good when trust is eroded. Trust is so fragile that it can be easily destroyed by social corruption, which alarms individuals that others are not adhering to shared ethical standards, including those in authority and positions of power (Fukuyama, 1995).

How Social Corruption Erodes Trust

Nepotism, favoritism, and the manipulation of social institutions are a few manifestations of social corruption. Individuals and groups lose faith in the fairness and integrity of their society when they perceive that rules and norms are being subverted by corruption. They lose their faith and trust when social corruption involves institutions that are supposed to embody justice, equality, and the common good, such as the legal system, educational institutions, and religious organizations (Rothstein, 2011).

Social corruption mainly occurs when nepotism and favoritism dominate hiring practices, educational admissions, or the distribution of public resources, and people believe that success is determined by connections and bribes and not by merit or hard work. This perception disregards the principle of fairness and discourages hard work, investment in education, careers, or civic participation as they feel the system is rigged. Disillusionment can lead to apathy, disengagement, or even active resistance to social norms and laws (Uslaner, 2002).

There are also cases of manipulation of religious institutions for personal or political gain that can severely erode trust. Religious institutions are among the most trusted and revered institutions in many societies, as they often serve as moral and ethical guides. However, religious supporters and believers can experience a crisis of faith when religious leaders engage in embezzling funds, selling religious offices, or aligning themselves with corrupt figures and such practices. The disillusionment of the believers toward their religious institutional leaders can spill over into a broader distrust of all social institutions and the overall erosion of trust in society (Philp, 1997).

Historical Examples of Social Corruption and Trust Erosion

A recurring theme in the decline of civilizations is marked by the decline of trust due to social corruption. The most famous example of social corruption in history is the downfall of the Roman Empire, where social corruption played a devastating role in eroding public trust. The Roman elites increasingly engaged in bribery, nepotism, and abuse of public offices as the Empire expanded. These and other forms of corrupt practices eroded the trust of the Roman citizens in their leaders and institutions, slowly fragmenting the Empire and eventually leading to its collapse (Syme, 1939).

This form of corruption is still happening in this modern period, which has a concrete case during the late Middle Ages with the Catholic Church as one of the religious institutions in Europe. The widespread disillusionment among the faithful led to the Protestant Reformation and centuries of religious conflict and social upheaval across Europe (Luther, 2003).

Recently, the erosion of trust due to social corruption can be observed in many developing countries where nepotism, favoritism, and bribery are endemic. Social corruption in this context has resulted in complex challenges for governments in implementing effective policies, maintaining social order, or achieving sustainable development due to a lack of trust in the institutions (Rose-Ackerman & Palifka, 2016).

The Long-Term Consequences of Eroded Trust

Due to social corruption, the erosion of trust in institutions has produced long-term negative consequences for the stability and prosperity of societies. Once trust is lost, it can be challenging to restore as the social contract between people and their institutions is fundamentally damaged.

This mistrust can lead to a vicious cycle where corruption breeds various corruptors and corrupt activities, as individuals feel justified in involving in corrupt practices in response to the perceived or experienced corruption of others (Uslaner, 2002).

Furthermore, due to the erosion of trust, individuals and groups become more isolated and less willing to cooperate, leading to the breakdown of social cohesion. The resulting fragmented society will find it very challenging to address collective difficulties, such as economic inequality, environmental degradation, or political instability. In some instances, the erosion of trust is the main factor that brings social instability and the emergence of conflicts, and individuals and groups resort to violence and other means to fulfill their goals (Fukuyama, 1995).

Conclusion

Social corruption and the erosion of trust are interconnected and play a crucial role in the decline of civilizations. When corruption infiltrates social institutions, it sabotages ethical norms and values, which could lead to disillusionment and the breakdown of social cohesion. Great civilizations of the past and contemporary societies illustrate how the erosion of trust due to social corruption can contribute to the decline of societies. Addressing social corruption and restoring trust requires advanced governance, anti-corruption measures, and a commitment to upholding ethical standards and fostering social cohesion.

References

Acemoglu, D., & Robinson, J. A. (2012). *Why Nations Fail: The Origins of Power, Prosperity, and Poverty.* Crown Business.

Friedman, E., Johnson, S., Kaufmann, D., & Zoido-Lobatón, P. (2000). *Dodging the grabbing hand: The determinants of unofficial activity in 69 countries.* Journal of Public Economics, 76(3), 459-493.

Fukuyama, F. (1995). *Trust: The Social Virtues and the Creation of Prosperity.* Free Press.

Huang, R. (1996). *China: A Macro History.* M.E. Sharpe.

Jones, A. H. M. (1964). *The Later Roman Empire, 284–602: A Social, Economic, and Administrative Survey.* Johns Hopkins University Press.

Levi, M. (1997). *Consent, Dissent, and Patriotism.* Cambridge University Press.

Luther, M. (2003). *Martin Luther's Basic Theological Writings.* Fortress Press.

Mauro, P. (1995). Corruption and growth. *The Quarterly Journal of Economics, 110*(3), 681–712.

North, D. C. (1990). *Institutions, Institutional Change, and Economic Performance.* Cambridge University Press.

Philip, M. (1997). Defining Political Corruption. *Political Studies, 45*(3), 436–462.

Putnam, R. D. (2000). *Bowling Alone: The Collapse and Revival of American Community.* Simon & Schuster.

Rose-Ackerman, S. (1999). *Corruption and Government: Causes, Consequences, and Reform.* Cambridge University Press.

Rose-Ackerman, S., & Palifka, B. J. (2016). *Corruption and Government: Causes, Consequences, and Reform.* Cambridge University Press.

Ross, M. L. (2012). *The Oil Curse: How Petroleum Wealth Shapes the Development of Nations.* Princeton University Press.

Rothstein, B. (2011). *The Quality of Government: Corruption, Social Trust, and*

Inequality in International Perspective. University of Chicago Press.

Shleifer, A., & Vishny, R. W. (1993). *Corruption.* The Quarterly Journal of Economics, 108(3), 599-617.

Syme, R. (1939). *The Roman Revolution. Oxford University Press.*

Uslaner, E. M. (2002). *The Moral Foundations of Trust.* Cambridge University Press.

World Bank. (2020). *World Development Report 2020: Trading for Development in the Age of Global Value Chains.* World Bank Publications.

ABOUT THE AUTHOR

Abbey Abramson is a dedicated expert in corruption and transparency, with a multidisciplinary academic background that includes degrees in psychology, theology, linguistics, and international development. His work, rooted in an understanding of human behavior, ethics, communication, and global systems, has been instrumental in promoting integrity and accountability across various sectors.

As an affiliate of a leading international anti-corruption NGO, Abbey has contributed to policy development, capacity building, and advocacy initiatives. He has collaborated with governments, civil society organizations, and private sector stakeholders to design and implement effective anti-corruption frameworks. His efforts focus on empowering individuals and institutions to uphold principles of fairness and accountability, driving meaningful change in the fight against corruption.